IMAGES
of America

THE OLD SPANISH TRAIL HIGHWAY IN TEXAS

Oliver "Dad" Holloway operated Dad's Filling Station in Weimar, Texas, on a 24-hour basis in the late 1920s and early 1930s (the truck is a 1929 Ford Model A), serving late-night travelers passing through on the Old Spanish Trail Highway. The large sign on the roof guided drivers to him. This charming postcard and the distinct "rest room" signs all spoke of a family-friendly business. (Nesbitt Memorial Library Archives.)

ON THE COVER: By the late 1930s, most of the Old Spanish Trail (OST) Highway was paved through the Texas Hill Country. Russell Lee recorded this 1939 view into Junction. Lee was part of a photography team working for the Farm Security Administration charged with recording life in rural communities during the Depression years when the OST became a major route for both auto tourists and unemployed families in search of work. (Library of Congress.)

IMAGES
of America

THE OLD SPANISH TRAIL HIGHWAY IN TEXAS

James Collett

ARCADIA
PUBLISHING

Published by Arcadia Publishing
Charleston, South Carolina

Printed in the United States of America

Library of Congress Control Number: 2021939289

For all general information, please contact Arcadia Publishing:
Telephone 843-853-2070
Fax 843-853-0044
E-mail sales@arcadiapublishing.com
For customer service and orders:
Toll-Free 1-888-313-2665

Visit us on the Internet at www.arcadiapublishing.com

To all who dwelt along the trail, to those dedicated to preserving its memory, and to those who have yet to discover the joy of traveling it.

Contents

ACKNOWLEDGMENTS

One of the great pleasures of researching this book was connecting with so many other people who find the Old Spanish Trail Highway as fascinating as I do. Like me, many of them grew up along the Texas portion of the route or have become residents there. I found them to be unvaryingly helpful in my quest for information, contacts, images, and information. Without them, this book would not have been possible. Like the OST itself, the book depended upon collaboration among a diverse collection of communities and people for its success. Among those to whom I owe thanks are the National Archives; Library of Congress Prints and Photograph Division; Special Collections and University Archives, St. Mary's University, San Antonio (Dr. Lindsey Weick, librarian Jill Crane, and Gloria Turnbull); Collection of the St. Augustine Historical Society Research Library, St. Augustine, Florida; Nesbitt Memorial Library Archives, Columbus (Susan Chandler, director); Special Collections, University of Texas at San Antonio (Carlos Cortez); Heritage House Museum, Orange; Sam Houston Regional Library and Research Center, Liberty; Tyrrell Historical Library, Beaumont; Caroline Wadzeck, Dayton; Houston Public Library Digital Archives, Houston; Fort Bend County Libraries Genealogy & Local History Department, Richmond; Fort Bend Museum, Richmond; E.A. Arnim Archives and Museum, Flatonia (Judy Pate); Seguin Guadalupe County Heritage Museum, Seguin; Old Spanish Trail Centennial Celebration Association, San Antonio (Charlotte Kahl); Comfort Heritage Foundation (Bryden Moon and Margaret Morries); Kimble County Historical Museum, Junction (Connie Sue Low); Texas Department of Transportation; Sutton County Historical Society, Sonora; Texas State Library and Archives, Austin; Portal to Texas History, Denton; Texas Historical Commission (Jefferson Spilman and Fort Lancaster); J. Wayne Holmes, Arlington; Fort Stockton Historical Society (Annie Riggs and memorial museum director Melba Montoya); Pecos County Historical Commission (Ernest Woodward, Kirby Warnock, and the late Kellie Templeton); Texas Parks and Wildlife (Chase Fountain); the Clark Hotel Museum, Van Horn (Patricia Golden); and Warren Nutt, Pecos County.

INTRODUCTION

At the dawn of automobile travel in America, a group of visionary entrepreneurs gathered in Mobile, Alabama, in December 1915. These pioneers proposed the bold idea of constructing a southern interstate route connecting Florida's east coast with New Orleans to draw more tourists into the region. They christened their projected road "the Old Spanish Trail Highway," embodying the idea of linking the historic communities of St. Augustine, Florida, and New Orleans, Louisiana.

By July 1919, at the organization's meeting in Houston, Texas, a grander vision had emerged—a road stretching from coast to coast, connecting through historic cities with Spanish ties (San Antonio, El Paso, and Tucson) and ending in San Diego, California. This highway, familiarly abbreviated as the OST, could become the nation's shortest "all weather and all year" transcontinental highway. Over 900 miles of Texas comprised the central third of this proposed road.

At the Houston conference, the association created a new headquarters in San Antonio's Gunter Hotel, a landmark anchor of that city's center. In November 1919, the Old Spanish Trail Highway board of directors hosted a well-attended San Antonio convention, with highway enthusiasts arriving from as far as Florida and California.

The group fortunately found the ideal man to lead the organization, without whom the unprecedented venture might have failed. After a successful financial career in New York associating with Wall Street giants such as the J.P. Morgan Company, Harral Ayres left the northeast in 1917 seeking to improve his health. Traveling west, Ayres halted in San Antonio for a bit of leisure. The chamber of commerce recruited him in 1919 to manage the development of the proposed transcontinental highway.

Ayres tirelessly promoted the road, traveling extensively, collecting historical data, drafting a wealth of promotional literature, and forming invaluable connections from the federal to the local level. Supported by an executive board of San Antonio businessmen and OST members from all eight states along the route, Ayres developed support cadres among businessmen and civic leaders in communities large and small across Texas. This network provided travelers with the comfort of knowing a representative of the Old Spanish Trail system awaited them to provide information, directions, or assistance when they arrived tired and road-weary. The organization developed unique signage and route guidance for motorists, all in the distinctive red and yellow colors of the Spanish flag.

The OST association strongly advocated for federal, state, and local funding to construct and improve roads, and worked in tandem with the development of the national highway system. When Pres. Woodrow Wilson signed the Federal Aid Road Act of 1916 providing federal funding to states to develop public roads, Texas responded by creating the Texas Highway Commission the following year and designing a statewide network of proposed highways.

The exact path of the Old Spanish Trail Highway remained undetermined at that time, with several options under consideration. Texas Route 3, designated the "Southern National Highway," included what became the eastern segment of the trail. The eager support of a network of small

Texas towns led Ayres and his board to favor a route from San Antonio stretching through the Texas Hill Country then west across the Trans-Pecos to El Paso, despite the primitive road conditions. The Texas Highway Commission meanwhile had assigned various highway numbers. The Texas portion of the Old Spanish Trail included segments of State Highways 3, 9, and 10.

With the Texas portion of the Old Spanish Trail Highway defined, Ayres began the hard work of making the trail a reality. In 1922, he lobbied in Washington, DC, for federal support. His efforts paid off. The Old Spanish Trail Highway was declared a basic trunk line, making it eligible for federal funding. In August of that year, the War Department declared it a military necessity of the first importance, and General of the Armies John J. Pershing placed it on his "Development of National Highways" map.

Ayres and fellow association members worked to create a unique identity for the OST to link "the playgrounds of Florida with the playgrounds of California" and fuel a constant flow of travel and commerce. Ayres extensively researched the Spanish history of the region, publicizing it through press releases, association publications, and historical plaques at official hotels along the route. A beautification campaign focused on the removal of billboards, planting of trees and shrubs, widening roadways, and developing auto camps.

By 1920, as American ownership of automobiles became commonplace, the first wave of motor tourism was underway. In these early years of long-distance recreational automobile travel, families navigated rugged, ill-defined roads with few amenities along the way. Autocamping, converting the car into a nightly campsite, became a popular fad. Many "tin can tourists" traveled the Old Spanish Trail, with a few even attempting the entire transcontinental journey. Texas, the central portion of the trail, benefited from this two-way stream of cars, goods, and people.

To aid these highway pioneers, Ayers and the association produced annual *Travelogs* between 1923 and 1931, over 62,000 of them, providing detailed information about the route. In addition, Ayres helped write and produce 60,000 other publications and 10,000 lithographed wall maps.

Throughout the 1920s, work continued along the route, with construction efforts from the local to the national level. Graveling, asphalt paving, bridge construction, and even improving dirt roads all were underway as the number of travelers grew. In 1926, federal highway designations were assigned, with the Texas portion of the OST following US Highways 90, 290, and 80. By 1928, the entire route was an official US highway.

Despite state and federal numbered roadways beginning to eclipse named highways, the OST retained its identity. As new forms of roadside business arose, local communities frequently drew on the OST heritage, branding businesses with elements of Ayres's research.

In 1929, the OST association declared the highway complete from coast to coast. $70 million had been expended in building the paved and graveled (with few exceptions) road. Another $40 million would be required to pave those exceptions. The "all weather and all year transcontinental highway" conceived a decade earlier now existed. In celebration, a 1929 caravan of vehicles traveled the entire route from San Diego to St. Augustine, covering 5,800 miles in 23 days in what was billed at the time as the longest motorcade ever attempted.

For the next 50 years, the OST continuously changed, transforming from a small named roadway into multi-lane Interstate 10, carrying an increasing flow of goods, services, and people. Texans dwelling beside the Trail or traveling it lived through dramatic decades of change, including the rise and fall of the service station industry, the transition of lodging from campgrounds to motor courts to motels, the proliferation of mom-and-pop tourist enterprises, and the coming of chains and standardization to even the smaller communities.

As the centennial of the Old Spanish Trail Highway's development arrived, a nostalgic initiative to remember and recreate some of those early days began, encouraging new generations of Texans to retrace the original route and rediscover the treasures Harold Ayres described in his 1920 poem "The Creed of the Trail": "Along the Old Spanish Trail are the riches of history, legend, sentiment and natural beauty. Don't hurry!"

One

BLAZING THE TRAIL

When the founders of what became the Old Spanish Trail Highway met in Mobile, Alabama, there were no highways in the United States. Most existing roads were local paths for horse-drawn vehicles. Long-distance travel was primarily by railroad. Yet the growing numbers of automobiles in the country and the desire to drive them farther than the next community heralded the future. The Good Roads movement encouraged better-connected routes, and auto-trail groups such as the OST organization promoted the construction of improved pathways across the nation.

Representatives from Texas were among 419 chamber of commerce officials, good roads advocates, politicians, newspapermen, and the simply curious attending the December 1915 convention as delegates. Filled with fire and determination, they had a vision of a southern route connecting the Atlantic and Pacific coasts. Harry Locke, a Los Angeles highway "pathfinder" and mapmaker, even presented a potential highway route from Houston to Los Angeles. Yet no one in that 1915 gathering had an inkling that the dream would require 14 years and over $70 million to achieve.

Texas would have to play a significant role in any southern transcontinental road. However, beyond two major rail lines across the state—the Texas & Pacific and the Southern Pacific—Texas remained a largely rural region with much of its attention focused on the chaos across the border in Mexico. Building an automobile route for over 900 miles through a terrain of coastal plains, rivers, mountains, and deserts would not be easy.

There were, however, forces encouraging this effort. The rapidly expanding petroleum industry helped fuel the Texas drive for highways. Texas was among the first to form a highway department to take advantage of federal highway funds. In 1919, when the OST headquarters relocated to Texas, the state became the leader in turning the Old Spanish Trail Highway into reality.

Enthusiasm outran plans for the OST path across Texas. This 1917 map included no definitive route. Two options wound to Dallas, then followed the Texas & Pacific Railroad to El Paso. While the lower route to Houston followed what became the East Texas segment, San Antonio, the hub of Spanish Texas, did not appear on the map. (Old Spanish Trail Association Archives, St. Mary's University.)

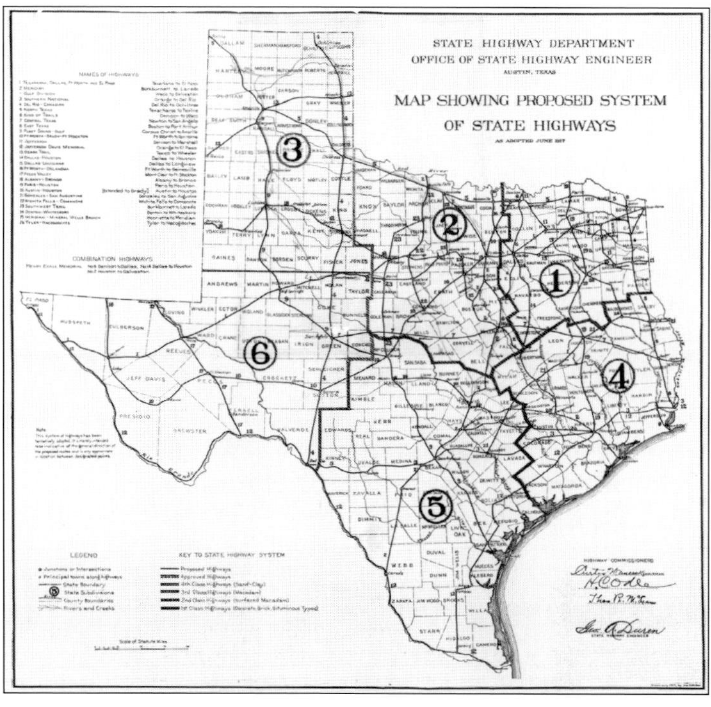

The first state highways map proposed by the Texas Highway Commission in 1917, the year of its founding, reflected the uncertainty regarding the Texas OST path. The Old Spanish Trail does not appear on the map. State Highway 3 was designated the Southern National and ran west from San Antonio to Del Rio. No highway was specified through the Texas Hill Country from San Antonio to Sonora. (Texas Historical Commission.)

By 1919, Texas was central to the OST organization. At the July conference in Houston, the organization voted to move its headquarters to the Gunter Hotel in downtown San Antonio (depicted here on a 1919 postcard). The November San Antonio conference collected pledges from Texas cities. A network of councilors in every community along the route would advise travelers regarding road conditions and local accommodations. (James Collett.)

Recruited in 1919 as managing director of the Old Spanish Trail Association, Harral Ayres spent the next decade working tirelessly promoting the highway. He journeyed across Texas gaining community support from business and civic leaders. He conducted extensive historical research, incorporating it into numerous promotional works. In 1930, he received a medal from Spain, making him a knight of the Spanish king. (Old Spanish Trail Association Archives, St. Mary's University.)

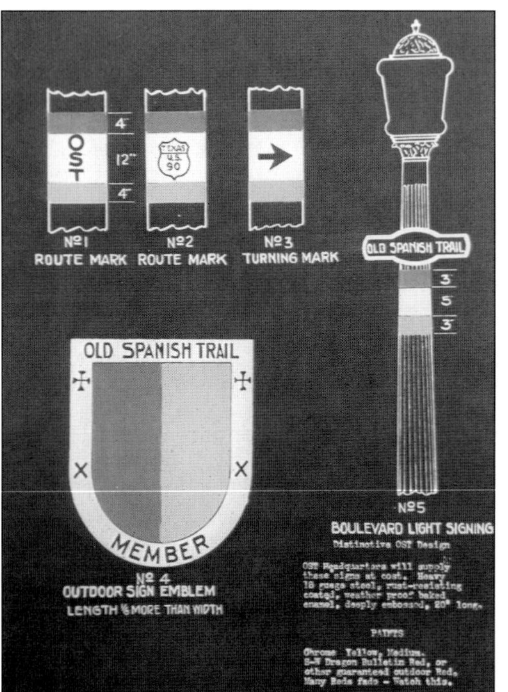

Early-1920s highway markings were primitive or nonexistent. The OST organization developed distinctive signage to help travelers along the route. Drawing on colors from the Spanish flag, route posts (often including direction arrows and highway designations) displayed bands of gloss white, bordered by chrome yellow and dragon red. As seen in this original drawing, branding extended to decorative signposts and shields. (Old Spanish Trail Association Archives, St. Mary's University.)

Signage reinforced Ayres's historical research on the Spanish Southwest in travel guides and publications promoting "the Creed of the Trail." Travelers were urged to respect the landscape. Local groups, especially women, supported his beautification program of roadside planting and removal of billboards and commercial signage. In this photograph, an unidentified group gathers around an OST-marked lamppost along a street bordered with palms. (Old Spanish Trail Association Archives, St. Mary's University.)

Constructing the Texas highways required years of work by counties and, later, the Texas Highway Department. Road quality varied dramatically, from shell roads to sand and clay to gravel and dirt. Some of the earliest paving of the OST route utilized rock asphalt (like this fist-sized piece) quarried at Uvalde, Texas. The rock was naturally saturated with asphalt from ancient volcanic activity. The quarry remains in use today. (James Collett.)

The OST association pronounced the transcontinental highway completed in 1929. A motorcade embarked from San Diego on March 23, traveling 2,743 miles to St. Augustine. On April 3, a zero stone marking the highway's beginning point was dedicated. Here, Ayres stands beside his car next to the Florida stone in the lead position of the return motorcade to California's zero stone. (St. Augustine Historical Society Research Library.)

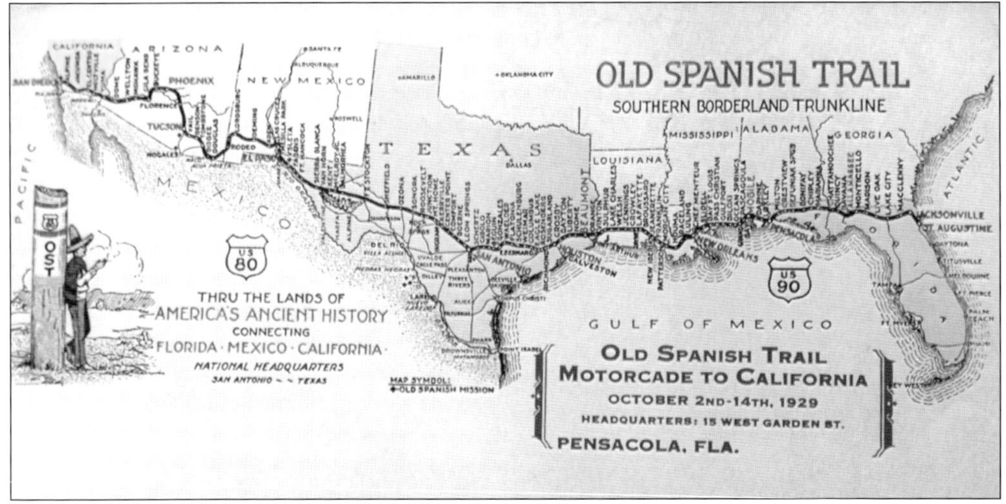

The map accompanying the October 1929 motorcade from Florida to California detailed the "completed" Old Spanish Trail Highway, identifying communities along the route. While some sections remained little more than dirt roads, others improved significantly throughout the 1930s. As more motorists ventured onto the OST, tourist-based businesses—gasoline stations and garages, tourist camps and courts, restaurants and grocers—developed to serve them. (Old Spanish Trail Association Archives, St. Mary's University.)

From the early 1920s, diverse travelers set out upon the road Ayres described, including wealthy autocampers, middle-class tourists, migrants, families, loners, short trippers, and coast-to-coasters. Among the more unusual was Col. Raymond Garner, a former US Army scout and "Official Trail Blazer" of the Old Spanish Trail, riding east from San Diego, seen here in December 1929 in Columbus, Texas. (Nesbitt Memorial Library Archives.)

Two

Crossing East Texas

With the end of the Great War in Europe and the waning of the influenza epidemic, many new automobile owners hungered to take to the highway. Twenty thousand Americans drove across the nation in 1921, many of them along the southern route.

Travelers crossing the vast expanse of Texas on the Old Spanish Trail Highway encountered a great variety of terrain, from bayous to arroyos, pine forests to deserts. They sought gasoline, supplies, and lodging in Texas communities ranging from small towns to large cities. Some were enticed to stop for sightseeing, camping, and other local attractions. Others traveled long, weary miles toward their destinations, wondering if they would ever get out of the state.

Those arriving from the east first found familiar terrain. Entering Texas over the Sabine River, drivers crossed a coastal plain intersected by numerous rivers and bayous, arriving at the metropolis of Houston a hundred miles later. Expanses of rice fields and grazing cattle gave way to booming oil fields and busy ports.

In the early years of the 1920s, roads and amenities often proved primitive. Gasoline pumps began as curbside additions to garages and related businesses, later evolving into service stations. Lodging choices were limited. Hotels originally designed for railroad travelers often proved ill-suited to automobile passengers unkempt from hours on the road. Municipal campgrounds developed to serve "tin-can tourists" who favored more rugged accommodations. Commercial camp courts and tourist courts developed as the rudimentary beginnings of the motel trade.

From its founding, the OST organization worked to assist these pioneers of the open road. Even smaller Texas towns had designated councilors to provide directions. Beginning in 1923, annual *Travelogs* detailed everything from road conditions and local businesses to the amenities of the public tourist camps.

East Texas counties worked in conjunction with the new Texas highway department to build and constantly improve the OST, soon designated US Highway 90, across their region. Communities of all sizes added their own style of Texas hospitality to the nationally emerging industries of tourist courts, motor hotels, and gasoline stations.

In the early 1920s, travelers entering Texas along the Old Spanish Trail arrived the same way as early settlers, by ferry. Instead of wagons, the Louisiana Highway Department ferry between Vinton, Louisiana, and Orange, Texas, carried automobiles. In 1925, the ferry operated from 5:00 a.m. to midnight. Rates were 75¢ to $1. Repeated river crossings defined the journey across East Texas—five rivers in 40 miles. (UTSA Special Collections.)

Bridging the three-mile-wide Sabine River and marsh proved among the most challenging projects of the Old Spanish Trail Highway. The cost rose to $700,000 before its 1927 completion. On November 11 of that year, cars and pedestrians streamed across the Orange and Calcasieu Memorial Bridge beneath flag and banner-draped girders. Ayres pronounced it "one of the big works" of the highway. (Heritage House Museum.)

16

Truss bridges, like the Sabine River one seen here, became familiar sights along the Texas OST. Their triangular metal elements and concrete worked in compression and tension to carry heavier loads. The 1927 OST travel bulletin reported, "No ferries in Texas." River crossings no longer presented a major barrier to the flow of tourists, except when the unpredictable rivers rose too high in floods. (Heritage House Museum.)

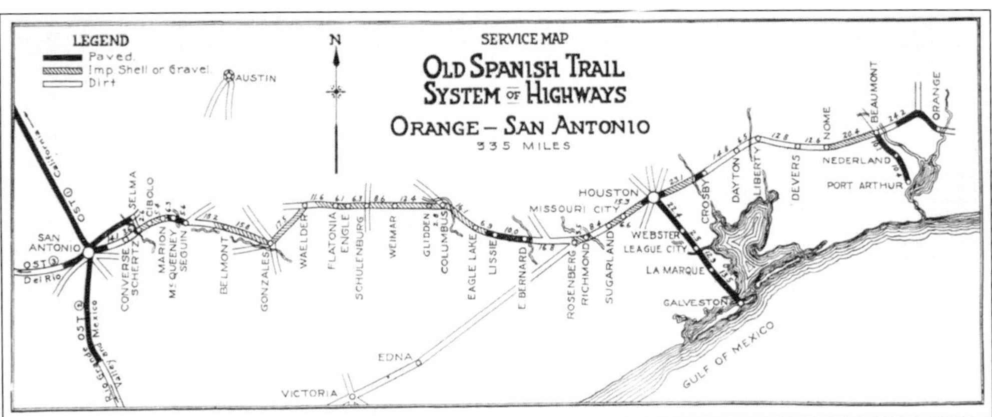

The OST association produced a *Travelog* series between 1923 and 1931. Each provided detailed information on the existing road, highway construction details, mileage between communities, and accounts of local historical events and sites. The 1923 edition included segment maps accompanying the text. This one, showing details from the Texas border to San Antonio, helped travelers make more realistic plans for daily travel and overnight stops. (OST100 *Travelog* collection.)

The Texas Highway Department entered the information business in 1936, creating "information houses" across the state, especially at border entry points. The "house" in Orange used a log cabin style to create a pioneer feel. A large shield sign included an outline of the state. At 13 of these stops, Texas A&M University cadets handed out some of the first widely distributed Texas travel maps. (Heritage House Museum.)

In 1936, Texas launched a centennial celebration that drew some six million visitors to the state. The following year, stone markers featuring the outline of Texas were placed at state entry points. Arriving visitors frequently stopped at the distinctive markers for a family photograph. This marker on Green Avenue in Orange demonstrated their sturdiness by surviving the 1953 flooding of the Sabine River. (Heritage House Museum.)

OST travelers frequently arrived seeking one or more travel necessities, especially gasoline. The growth in automobile traffic inspired bicycle shops, car garages, and even auto dealers to install gasoline pumps on the street outside their establishments. In this photograph from around 1920, motorcyclists pose outside the Exide Battery and Service Station in Orange, the gasoline pump sharing curb space with the barbershop pole. (Heritage House Museum.)

Businesses devoted to supplying gasoline developed along busier travel routes. Many were rudimentary roadside stops, with little distinguishing them beyond a canopy and pumps. Gasoline name branding lay in the future. Some, however, such as the Log Cabin Station, on Green Avenue near the state bridge, sought more identity, drawing on East Texas pioneer roots. In this 1929 photograph, even the pumps seem to resemble tree stumps. (Heritage House Museum.)

Gasoline stations soon developed branding and standard architecture under the influence of major oil companies. Three major companies—the Texas Company, Gulf Oil, and Humble—formed during the first East Texas oil boom in 1901. By 1930, this Gulf station at the intersection of Green Avenue and Fifth Street in Orange had international-style architecture, uniformed attendants, and amenities such as air, water, and Supreme motor oil. (Heritage House Museum.)

Petroleum was plentiful in East Texas. Following the 1901 Spindletop gusher, a rush to develop new oil-producing fields made this region a center of petroleum production and refining. As the OST developed, so did new oil fields east of Orange. Orangefield boomed through much of the 1920s, as seen in this 1922 photograph. Pioneer OST travelers saw firsthand a mythic Texas image—a forest of oil derricks. (Heritage House Museum.)

In the early 1920s, most communities, especially along major railroad routes, had commercial hotels, largely occupied by drummers and other businessmen and catering primarily to men's needs. Orange's Holland Hotel, built in the early 1900s, had 100 rooms. Sixty had their own bath, a rarity that might make it more acceptable to family travelers at the end of a long day of driving. (Heritage House Museum.)

As automobile travel grew, hotels restructured, becoming more accommodating to families arriving a bit disheveled from a day on the road. Some began advertising annually in the OST *Travelogs*. By the 1930s, travelers turning down Fifth Street in Orange to reach the Holland entered a busy thoroughfare where they could purchase a variety of supplies from hardware to sodas to groceries at the Piggly Wiggly. (Heritage House Museum.)

In the early days of the OST, autocamping became a fad. Travelers stopped along the roadside or in community campgrounds. These "tin can tourists" cooked their own meals, converting automobiles into dining facilities and lodging for the evening. Traveling economically, they enjoyed reliving the pioneer experience. Dr. A.A. Foster and family from Dallas relax with their elaborate setup in a Washington, DC, camp. (James Collett.)

Many communities set up public campgrounds, charging little or no fee for a spot. Local entrepreneurs later entered the market, competing with additional amenities. Edna and Bob Dillard of Orange probably left town to camp, but the Orange tourist facility generously included tables, benches, ovens, toilets, shower baths, and running water. In the 1930s, the increase of migrant families led towns to raise rates, discouraging longer stays. (Heritage House Museum.)

For the autocamper requiring a new auto to embark on or continue their OST journey, Hill Motor Company of Orange stood ready to provide a new Ford. In this 1918 photograph, 11 new Fords line up in front of the dealership. Palm trees along the curb add an extra touch of distinction. Dealers might also be a sole source for critical repairs for long-distance travelers. (Heritage House Museum.)

By the late 1920s, the year-round touring season and high proportion of affluent cross-country tourists created a new industry—the motor court. Like the Orange Grande Courts on Highway 90 West, they consisted of separate cabin units with hotel-level equipment: indoor plumbing, stucco or brick construction, sofas, appliance-equipped kitchenettes, and an attached garage for the automobile. Some also included a restaurant and gasoline station on the property. (Heritage House Museum.)

After 1938, before departing Orange, travelers could visit and drive across a bigger-in-Texas engineering feat. The bridge arching across the Neches River between Orange and Port Arthur was the South's tallest, rising 176 feet above the water. Over 7,300 feet in length, it was renamed the Rainbow Bridge in 1957 based upon its shape. (James Collett.)

This early postcard of the OST depicted a rosy picture of smooth traveling in beautiful weather. Drivers in 1924 had pavement within three miles of Beaumont. Over the next 90 miles, the route became improved with shell, gravel, and even dirt at times. While things improved markedly over the next few years, the work was expensive and slow, impeded by numerous river and drainage problems. (Sam Houston Regional Library and Research Center.)

The reality of 1920s travel
across East Texas proved
quite challenging. Dirt
roads quickly became
quagmires in wet weather,
as these drivers near Orange
learned. Even when the
highway conditions were
good, exits for camping
or lodging became
problematic. By 1930, the
OST, designated State
Highway 3 and US Highway
90, was paved (asphalt,
brick, concrete, or surface
treated) from the Louisiana
border to Houston.
(Heritage House Museum.)

Flooding could create hazardous travel. On the night of May 17, 1923, the Beaumont area received
13.5 inches of rain in two hours. The Neches River rose 11 feet overnight. This was the scene the
following day at Pipkin and Brulin Company Magnolia Service Station, at the corner of Pearl
and Broadway Streets in Beaumont. The damage to Beaumont buildings and homes reached an
estimated $1 million. (Tyrrell Historical Library.)

Road construction required a collaborative effort between county and state. Early 1920s work sometimes relied on horse-drawn Fresno scrapers. The Neches River Bridge at Beaumont opened in May 1925, a 25-foot-high embankment carrying the highway above cypress swamps. Beaumont was part of the Golden Triangle along with Orange and Port Arthur, a booming oil and refining region in the 1920s and 1930s. (James Collett.)

Beaumont's Crosby Hotel offered more elegant lodging than the tourist camp at the city fairgrounds. The city's leading hospice during the 1901 Spindletop oil boom, the Crosby was renovated in the fall of 1922 by the Daley-Moffatt Hotel Company of Houston, owners of several area hotels. For guests entering the redecorated lobby, resident manager J.M. Purcell offered "Courtesy— Hospitality—Service," with rates beginning at $1. (Tyrrell Historical Library.)

Beaumont's service stations included the Pure Oil Company, pictured in August 1939. Constructed in the English Cottage style patented by the company in the late 1920s, with a canopy addition for shade from the Texas heat, these stations conveyed the look of a private home, making them more acceptable in middle-class neighborhoods. H.L. Rocca's Beaumont Pep Station supplied Yale tires, Tiolene motor oil, and Pure gasoline. (Tyrrell Historical Library.)

By contrast, the 1930s Magnolia Station in the community of Amelia, a few miles west of Beaumont, occupied a high-visibility spot on a well-paved US Route 90. Located next to the Amelia Railroad Station, the business provided Magnolia gasoline and Mobilgas for both locals and OST travelers. Added enticements included Coca-Cola and a ladies' restroom. (Tyrrell Historical Library.)

Liberty County officials provided invaluable contributions to the construction of the OST across their county. Local businesses appreciated the effort. By the mid-1920s, E.G. Harrington, owner of Dayton's first car, operated Harrington's Garage on the corner of the OST and First Street in Dayton. Pictured from left to right are Toby Hansen, two unidentified, Milton Norcross, E.G. Harrington, R.I. Cleveland, Otto Harbeck, and unidentified. (Caroline Wadzeck.)

E.B. "Lett" Neuman ran this company-operated Magnolia service station along the OST route through Dayton. Magnolia Petroleum controlled 18 percent of the Texas gasoline market by 1926. Like its competitors, Magnolia attracted customers through distinctive branding. Neuman's sign and pumps contain magnolia blossoms, the original emblem of the company. This late 1920s photograph includes, from left to right, Lett Neuman, Joe Neuman, Kit Carson Neuman, and Jim Neuman. (Caroline Wadzeck.)

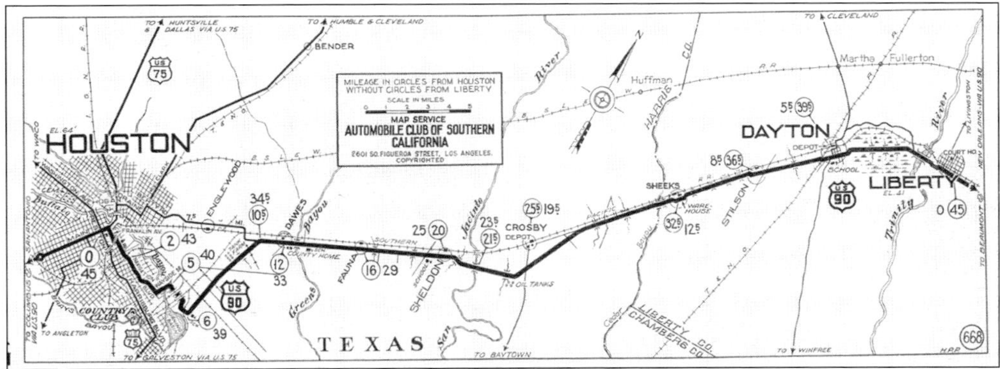

By 1930, gasoline companies such as Conoco provided foldout maps of Texas. Strip maps remained a popular form as well. The Automobile Club of Southern California published a 1933 book consisting of strip maps of the entire Old Spanish Trail Highway. The map segment on each page included mileage for travel in either direction and detailed street-level guidance for navigating larger communities and cities such as Houston. (James Collett.)

Beginning in 1936, OST travelers approaching Houston could see the obelisk of the San Jacinto Monument rising to the south. In this Works Progress Administration (WPA) photograph, workers are finishing the base. Completed in 1939, it rose 567 feet above the Texas landscape, topped with a 34-foot, 220-ton limestone, steel, and concrete star. Tourists with time for a side trip enjoyed the extensive view from atop the monument. (National Archives.)

The first Texas urban center on the OST, Houston, was daunting. Travelers made their way along Navigation Boulevard to Main Street then continued west. This 1930s downtown view includes several of the city's first skyscrapers. The Stowers Furniture Building, erected in 1913, stands right of Walker Street (center), with the Hotel Cotton to its right. Gulf Oil Company's 1929 Art Deco building is at far right. (Houston Public Library.)

Approaching a population of 300,000 in 1930, Houston had several quality hotels for the road-weary. When erected in 1913, the Hotel Cotton, among the city's first high rises, was borderline swank. Early ads touted its 175 fireproof rooms. Located at the southern edge of downtown, its other selling point was a bathroom in every room. In 1923, one of those rooms rented for $2 a night. (Houston Public Library.)

Though listed in OST guides, the Brazos was an opulent railroad hotel, as seen in this early 1900s lobby view. Designed for an earlier age of travelers, it served passengers arriving at Houston's Grand Central Station. Children were not allowed in the parlor, and ladies had to go upstairs to find a restroom. The Southern Pacific Station replaced the hotel in the early 1930s. (Houston Public Library.)

Although Houston's Main Street was paved, OST auto tourists might nostalgically recall a peaceful stretch of rural gravel. This 1930s view from Texas Avenue shows both the busy traffic and the myriad choices confronting a driver. On the left are the Rice Hotel, a clothing store, and a nearby bank. Across the street is Liggits Drug Store with a dentist's office above, and further down, Foley Brothers Department Store. (Houston Public Library.)

The Rice Hotel opened in 1913 on the site of the old capital of the Republic of Texas (1837–1839), Houston's tallest building at the time. The double-winged 17-story structure seen in this postcard was at the time the largest hotel in the South. The open-air roof contained beautiful gardens, and its cafeteria became Houston's first air-conditioned one. A third wing added in 1925 brought the room total to 1,000. (Houston Public Library.)

The 800 block of Houston's Main Street included the Bender Hotel on the left, constructed in 1911 with an ornate marble and brass interior. Amenities included a cafeteria, drugstore, and Turkish bath. A traffic signal tower can be seen in the center of the street. Originally manually operated to control traffic flow, automatic control of interconnected traffic lights was introduced in Houston in March 1922. (Houston Public Library.)

Early travelers seeking something between elegant downtown establishments and Houston's public campground to the west could choose the Lighthouse Tourist Tavern. Serving auto campers wishing to carry less gear, cabin camps offered more inexpensive touring vacations, with easy access, free parking, no reservations, and greater privacy than tent camping. It offered hot and cold baths, and patrons could choose to add mattresses, springs, and beds. (Houston Public Library.)

OST drivers seeking to refuel in the early 1920s could stop at the Texas Company Service Station No. 1, which opened in 1917 (seen here around 1919). The Texaco brand, with its logo of a red star with a green "T" in the center, was already prominent. The station promised free service. A sign at the pump added, "Customers will please not tip our employees." (Houston Public Library.)

In the 1920s, the Texas Company developed regional styles for its stations that reflected local architectural patterns. The Fontane station seen here used a Mission style designed for the Southwest resembling Hispanic stucco and adobe construction. Firestone tires received top billing over Texaco gas. For long-distance travelers needing a replacement, a station that also sold tires held a distinct advantage. (Houston Public Library.)

Drivers on the Old Spanish Trail Highway also encountered another feature of the growing automobile industry—trucks. Along with its advertising, this Esso truck included a polite offer to yield the right-of-way to motorists. Esso was one of the companies formed with the breakup of Standard Oil in 1911. The Esso brand was more common in Louisiana, with Humble being the brand name in Texas. (Houston Public Library.)

Three

REACHING SAN ANTONIO

From Houston, the Old Spanish Trail Highway ran east across the coastal plains, then along the northern edge of South Texas to reach San Antonio. Official highway designations were Texas Highway 3, and after 1927, US Highway 90.

The road meandered southwest to Richmond, northeast to Columbus, then generally west through Flatonia, dropping south again through Gonzales and Seguin, with a final dip to the southwest into San Antonio. The route traversed a historic region, its roots reaching back to early Anglo settlement in Texas. Richmond was listed as the state's first Anglo-American settlement, founded in the early years of the Republic of Texas. To the west, communities like Gonzales and Seguin reflected Mexican and Spanish origins.

In 1926, only one third of these approximately 200 miles were paved, the rest remaining dirt and gravel, some of it impassable in wet weather. A total of $2 million in investments that same year promised paving would go forward rapidly. In the meantime, the Motor League of South Texas worked diligently to get travelers through with reasonable comfort. By the early 1930s, paving was complete.

As drivers continued inland from the coast, they passed through farm and timberlands and open, grassy plains. A 1926 *Blue Book* added, "In places dense thickets of pecan groves line the highway and offer ideal camp sites." Local landowners, however, eventually grew weary of the refuse and damage often done by casual motor campers. Many closed their property to these "motor hoboes," especially as the Depression years drove people to migrate in search of work. Cities began imposing camping fees.

Finally, tourists arrived in San Antonio, a city steeped in history and a crossroads of Texas routes—northeast to Central and North Texas, south toward the Rio Grande Valley, and northwest into the Hill Country. Headquarters of the Old Spanish Trail Highway Association, the ancient Spanish capital offered numerous attractions. From old mission ruins to beautiful campgrounds and elegant hotels to the iconic Alamo, there was much to entice travelers to remain a while. Ayres suggested taking "plenty of time to see and enjoy."

Before the Brazos River Bridge opened at Richmond in 1925, automobiles crossed via the Richmond Ferry. P.J. Christensen recalled needing multiple efforts to get his Model T Ford up the steep west bank. The motor would die, rocks were quickly wedged behind the wheels to prevent it rolling backward, and then another attempt was made. Here, a baseball team poses during the crossing. (Fort Bend County Libraries Genealogy & Local History Department.)

Construction began on the Brazos River Bridge in 1922. In this photograph from the early days of the project, a crane works from a temporary steel structure to place the first set of concrete supports in the river. The completed bridge stood 46 feet above the water due to the significant floods of the river, which had proved devastating in the past. (Fort Bend Museum.)

Richmond residents turned out for the special events opening the Brazos River Bridge, which was decorated with banners and flags. Following the ceremonies, a grand party continued beneath the bridge with vendors selling refreshments, including 5¢ ice cream. A large banner atop the bridge proclaimed, "Welcome to Richmond. Use Imperial Sugar." Based in nearby Sugar Land, the Imperial Sugar Company was a major US sugar producer. (Fort Bend Museum.)

Much of Richmond's early 1900s business district grew up along Morton Street, serving the small agricultural community. The 1920s brought oil production and the OST. Civic improvements followed, including paved sidewalks and a tourist camp on the west side of town. In this undated photograph, perhaps from around 1920, businesses include a drugstore and the Rich Café. A Mobiloil sign is visible on the right. (Fort Bend Museum.)

To assist in "fostering the comfort and pleasure of travelers," the OST association appointed councilors living in communities along the highway. These local business and civic leaders provided information and guidance for floundering tourists. T.B. Wessendorf, a lumberyard owner and mayor from 1909 to 1924, served this role in Richmond. His elegant two-story Victorian home, seen here in 1901, was one of the city's showplaces. (Fort Bend Museum.)

Tom Wessendorf also provided help to motorists, albeit for a fee. He owned the Richmond Motor Car Company on Morton Street, an authorized Ford service station. For service repairs, drivers pulled into the garage (the door is on the far right). The 1924 OST guide listed the garage and included an important additional feature to traveling families—a ladies' restroom. (Fort Bend Museum.)

Once Highway 90 passed through Richmond along Jackson Street, gasoline stations sprang up along the road. By the time this 1930s photograph was taken, the road was paved, though the shoulders appear to remain dirt or gravel. Brand-name signs dominate. Station architecture varies, from house with canopy style (the Texaco station with attached garage on the right and Humble on the left) to oblong box (Gulf at far left). (Fort Bend Museum.)

Overnight travelers not wishing to camp had a choice of downtown hotels near the railroad. The National Hotel was the designated Richmond OST headquarters. Lodgers might learn of the hotel's claim to fame. In the late 1800s, the National was operated by David and Carrie Nation. After the family moved to Kansas, Carrie launched her temperance campaign and became famous for her hatchet-wielding exploits. (Fort Bend Museum.)

The rich black soil in the Richmond-Rosenberg area became virtually impassable in wet weather. Richmond suffered floods in 1922 and 1929. At the Harlem Prison Farm east of Richmond, officials stationed a guard and a convict with mules to pull motorists, like the family seen here, through the muck. This welcome courtesy probably also prevented tourists from falling victim to escaping convicts. (Fort Bend County Libraries Genealogy & Local History Department.)

City streets also proved challenging when wet. In this early 1920s view, the center of Third Street in Rosenberg has become a rutted mess (the city's earlier nickname was "city of mud"). The opening of oil fields in the area allowed for civic improvements, including a tourist camp in a mesquite grove on the east side of town complete with tables, benches, and toilets. (Fort Bend Museum.)

In good weather, the dirt roads of the South Texas prairies proved smooth to drive, though perhaps a bit dusty at times. This postcard of the road near Rosenberg includes a mention of the gulf breeze, implying a pleasant ride in a time before air conditioning through a rural landscape of rice, cotton farms, and cattle ranches. (Fort Bend County Libraries Genealogy & Local History Department.)

In winter, roads were firm but slick in a different manner. A layer of snow covers Rosenberg's Main Street in this photograph from the 1920s or 1930s. Travelers could get a hot cup of Sunset Coffee at the Eagle Café while having their cars serviced at the garage next door (far left). Syl and Carl Turricchi operated the Eagle Café from 1924 to 1932. (Fort Bend Museum.)

The 1925 OST *Travelog* listed a "country hotel and rooming house" for Rosenberg. This was most likely the two-story Victorian-style Plaza Hotel on Avenue F, seen here in a 1915 postcard. Travelers could choose the American plan (lodging and meals) for $2.50 per day or the more economical European plan (lodging only) for $1 per day and opt for a meal at the Eagle Café. (Fort Bend Museum.)

Twins Melvin and Marvin Reeh operated this Rosenberg Magnolia station on the corner of Avenue H and Second Street. Corner locations provided greater visibility and access. The 1920s Magnolia stations prominently advertised the full company name, but the roof and pumps Mobiloil signage points toward the later corporate name. Magnolia controlled 18 percent of the Texas markets, making their stations a regular sight. (Fort Bend County Libraries Genealogy & Local History Department.)

Rosenberg's R and L Filling Station took an interesting signage tack. The Texaco star is visible on the building, sign, and gas pumps, and there also appears to be a Mobiloil sign. However, the station name comes from the words "Right" and "Left," prominently painted on the front of the stucco canopy. Perhaps this unique take on the corner location reminded drivers of access from either direction. (Fort Bend Museum.)

The station in this January 1940 photograph displays highly eclectic options. An older wooden sign atop the canopy carries the motto, "That Good Gulf Gasoline." A rather plain Humble gasoline sign hangs in front. The pumps have different logos, and both General and Goodyear tire signs are visible. Drivers could also get "Free Crank Case Service," lunch, "Good Coffee," and "Smokes." (Fort Bend County Libraries Genealogy & Local History Department.)

By the 1930s, Rosenberg's Third Street was paved through a thriving business district. The OST Garage is on the far right, where "experienced mechanic" F.J. Jurica worked, according to the 1925 OST *Travelog*. While Jurica serviced their car, tourists could visit the OST Barber Shop next door for a haircut or a Dr. Pepper or cross the street for a movie at the Cole Theater. (Fort Bend Museum.)

By the date of this 1927 postcard, the road from Rosenberg to Eagle Lake contained "the first high class construction" of bridges and paving in the region. Downtown Eagle Lake had a beautiful square, complete with a bandstand. OST councilor W.E. Lenhart, a cashier at the First National Bank (center), was available for travelers needing information or directions to the tourist camp. (James Collett.)

The Haggley Brothers Camp Site Filling Station was near the Eagle Lake Tourist Camp east of town. The "filling station" sign with no gasoline brand indicates a 1920s date. The prominent "Ladies Rest Room" sign advertised an important accommodation. After filling up, campers found a site with screened sleeping rooms, showers, toilets, and ovens. (Nesbitt Memorial Library Archives.)

OST autocampers frequently carried cooking gear, purchasing groceries along the way. Oscar Miller's Q-P Store on Main Street in Eagle Lake (seen here in 1935) was well positioned to add autocampers to its clientele. Over time, campers began expecting better cooking amenities in campgrounds, especially fee-based ones. In the 1930s, families took to the road in search of work, and camping provided an affordable option. (Nesbitt Memorial Library Archives.)

Universal Motor Company and Garage was Eagle Lake's authorized Ford dealer (seen here around 1920). By the mid-1920s, a tire display such as this helped attract OST drivers needing replacements for road-worn tires. Universal sold both new and used Fords. A December 1929 Universal ad in the *Eagle Lake Headlight* listed a 1926 Model T touring car for $145. (Nesbitt Memorial Library Archives.)

The Colorado River Bridge is visible in this 1922 view from downtown Columbus. Gravel production was a major industry in the area, which made road construction affordable. Gravel man J.O. Tanner's name appears among the 1923 OST list of Columbus members. Highway 90 in 1920s Colorado County consisted of single-slab concrete 17.5 feet wide. A 1935 flood destroyed a portion of the bridge. (Nesbitt Memorial Library Archives.)

In 1922, the year of this photograph, James Wooten Jr. won the $10 prize for a new city slogan. His entry, "The city of live oaks and live folks," featured the moss-draped live oaks throughout the city. The second-largest live oak in Texas stood astride the OST route through town. The 1929 OST *Travelog* stated the Columbus autocamp included live oaks, conveniences, and several cabins. (Nesbitt Memorial Library Archives.)

OST travelers could purchase gasoline at a most unusual filling station in Columbus. In 1918, E.C. Guilmartin opened a Ford dealership and installed street-side gasoline pumps beside the Columbus Stafford Opera House, which closed in 1916. The second floor held the Grand Hall, which seated a thousand patrons. In 1926, Sam Harbert opened one of the first Dodge dealerships in Texas. (Nesbitt Memorial Library Archives.)

The Burt and Stafford Garage, built in 1919 by John Burt and Joe Stafford, housed a Chevrolet dealership, gasoline station, and garage on the Highway 90 route through Columbus. A Brunswick Tires sign gets top billing, far larger than the Texaco and Chevrolet signs. Charlie Stafford leans on a unique "Stop Here" sign. The seated garage crew and other men are unidentified. (Nesbitt Memorial Library Archives.)

While many Texaco service stations in Texas used a Mission look resembling stucco or adobe, this one in Columbus followed another Texas Company style. The house-and-canopy form demonstrates a Colonial Revival influence, with white wooden railing replacing the stucco. In this 1930s photograph, the lack of a large freestanding sign helps preserve the residential look and feel. (Nesbitt Memorial Library Archives.)

In September 1935, the original Columbus
Humble Oil Company gas station crew
(Justin Stein, Tommy Glithero, and
Clifford Leyendecker) pose for a portrait.
Humble stations built across Texas in the
1920s utilized a brick veneer construction
with a flat roof canopy and a single set
of pumps on a raised island. Humble
offered OST drivers a full complement of
products: gasoline, motor oils, and greases.
(Nesbitt Memorial Library Archives.)

Travelers headed west through Weimer
in the 1940s could pick up supplies at
the Herder Mercantile on the right and
stop for a bite at the gazebo in the park
on the left (across from the T.A. Hill
Bank, founded by Civil War veteran
Thomas Anderson Hill). The community
had grown since the 1920s, when it
provided a tourist camp with showers.
(Nesbitt Memorial Library Archives.)

Henry Brasher and his father, Henry Brasher Sr., opened a Buick dealership on Weimer's Main Street in 1915. When the OST route was established, the elder Brasher served as the Weimar OST councilor. Brasher Buick Garage (seen here on the left around 1945) offered toilets and ice water and continued to sell Texaco gasoline from a curbside pump. Brasher also owned Weimar's first telephone exchange. (Nesbitt Memorial Library Archives.)

Bob Adamick chose a unique advertising slogan for his Art Deco–style Schulenberg restaurant. Beneath his name on the building (and on his postcards), he claimed he provided "26-Hour" service. The Schulenberg tourist camp was originally located nearby. In 1922, over 500 cars carrying 18,000 people stopped at the supervised camp (and perhaps at Bob's café), which provided showers, toilets, tables and benches, ovens, wood, and a mailbox. (James Collett.)

Flatonia World War I veteran F.L. Wotipka was ahead of the competition as the OST developed across Fayette County. He established his Citizens Auto Supply in 1920 as an "up-to-date display and service garage" complete with a plate-glass front and tile floor. Wotipka's Ford dealership soon outgrew the building seen here in 1921. Wotipka established the Flatonia Motor Company on North Main Street. (E.A. Arnim Archives and Museum.)

In 1930, Charles Wolters and Benno Nierlich opened their "up-to-date" camp on east Main Street on the OST with four all-weather tourist quarters and a tourist garage for four automobiles. Their camp included the Flatonia Service Station (seen here in 1936), which provided three lines of gasoline and oils—Gulf, Texaco, and Magnolia—with a large "Cabins" sign instead of a gasoline brand. (E.A. Arnim Archives and Museum.)

Flatonia OST councilor O.L. Lee (right, with Eddie Zouzalik) constructed the corrugated-iron Lee and Vogt Garage in 1922. Lee was the first to seek a Texas Chevrolet dealership. The partners prospered, distributing 53 cars in October 1923. The 1925 OST *Travelog* promised a mechanic team that provided "careful attention." In 1931, Lee constructed a new 3,000-square-foot Lee Garage on Market Street. (E.A. Arnim Archives and Museum.)

Eddie Zouzalik became manager of the new standardized Gulf station in 1931, built adjacent to the Lee Garage. Flatonia represented a good example of how small Texas towns transformed into part of what the September 1934 *Fortune* magazine called "the great American roadside." Here, locals Herman Tauch (right), Arnold Tauch (center), and an unidentified man stop in. (E.A. Arnim Archives and Museum.)

Felix Brunner bought the Flatonia City Café in 1926 and catered to both locals and travelers. He represented another element of the American roadside: the restaurant. In this 1930s photograph, Frank Novak (far left) and Brunner serve customers. The fame of the café's delicious strawberry custard pie spread along the OST. Frequent travelers looked forward to returning for another slice, perhaps with a Coca-Cola. (E.A. Arnim Archives and Museum.)

The 1920s OST highway ran down Flatonia's North Main Street. Businesses like F.L. Wotipka's Flatonia Motor Company served any passing travelers who might have the need or desire to stop. Lacking significant landmarks, Flatonia businesses hoped the rolling countryside of well-kept farms might encourage motorists to travel a bit more leisurely to enjoy what the *Flatonia Argus* called "pleasing prosperity pictured poignantly." (E.A. Arnim Archives and Museum.)

Businesses quickly realized the benefit of billboard advertising along bustling highways. Dr. F.G. Daehne, owner of Flatonia's Daehne Drug Store, had an eye-catching windmill and large letters detailing items attractive to travelers. Floy Lee Berger, daughter of Flatonia grocer Ed Berger, added her 1920s charm to the sign. Billboards became regular OST features, enticing and directing tourists to a wide variety of attractions. (E.A. Arnim Archives and Museum.)

In this photograph from around 1930, Dr. Daehne's daughter Frances illustrates a common activity of travelers—taking their picture beside highway signs, in this case, one showing mileage east from Flatonia. Highway numbers, city limits, and mileage markers all became props to anchor a photograph's location in time and place. They also recorded the growing standardization of highway information first pioneered by the OST organization. (E.A. Arnim Archives and Museum.)

Drivers arriving at Seguin's "Four Corners" intersection in the 1930s could choose from stations on every corner, including the Magnolia station. The stucco-clad oblong-box structure was built in Spanish Colonial Revival style, with an arched opening under a gabled clay tile roof. These uniformed attendants were ready to provide service at the gasoline pumps or the garage bays on the right. (Seguin Guadalupe County Heritage Museum.)

The Seguin Park Hotel offered OST travelers an elegant stay. Built in 1917 by San Antonio businessman M.J. Dielman, the $75,000 hotel also contained several retail businesses and concessions. The building was the Seguin Hospital from 1927 to 1930, and then reopened as the Plaza Hotel. Those wishing a more rustic stay chose the tourist camp on the Guadalupe River with water, lights, fishing, and bathing. (James Collett.)

OST tourists approaching San Antonio encountered another developing roadside business—souvenir stands. This small curio stand displayed a collection of Mexican-style clay figures. Residents living alongside the highway constructed stands for a bit of extra income. This vendor may have had another revenue source. The sign partially visible on his stand advertised San Antonio's Grande Courts, among the first private businesses replacing public campgrounds (see page 60). (UTSA Special Collections.)

Arriving atop Rattlesnake Hill at the gates of Fort Sam Houston, OST travelers got a look at the San Antonio skyline, seen here around 1940. The second Texas OST urban center, San Antonio contained all the romantic elements glowingly described in the *Travelogs*: Spanish architecture, missions, aqueducts, and of course, the famous Alamo. There were beautiful parks and the first stages of the famed River Walk. (James Collett.)

Travelers with time and money discovered exciting possibilities in downtown 1930s San Antonio. The Old Spanish Trail National Headquarters was in the Gunter Hotel (left). Next door, the multicolored ornate Spanish Colonial–style arches of the Texas theater beckoned. The Majestic across the street, the first Texas theater to be fully air-conditioned, sported a 76-foot sign and a tropical fish aquarium in the lobby. (UTSA Special Collections.)

The Alamo, its iconic façade added long after the 1836 battle, was a must-see stop for visitors. In 1935, as part of the beautification project of Alamo Park, much of it done by WPA workers, the area in front of the building was paved with flagstone, and the rectangular lawn was created. The Crockett Hotel (seen behind the Alamo) advertised 122 rooms with private baths and free parking. (James Collett.)

The Menger Hotel, seen here in a 1917 postcard, stood beside the Alamo and was itself rich in historical associations. Built in 1859, Menger guests included Theodore Roosevelt (who recruited Rough Riders in the bar), the Irish poet Oscar Wilde, and baseball star Babe Ruth. After registering in the Victorian lobby, OST travelers could enjoy the view beneath "the most beautiful colonnade in the south." (James Collett.)

For those seeking a taste of Spanish heritage, Mission San Jose (founded in 1720), though a partial ruin in the 1920s, was open daily to visitors and held Sunday morning services in the sacristy. In 1938, following the Texas centennial, the old mission served as the set for *The Alamo: Shrine of Texas Liberty*, a film directed by Stuart Paton, produced in a couple of weeks. (James Collett.)

San Antonio's first luxury hotel, the St. Anthony, was built in 1909. By the mid-1920s, the 10-story hotel boasted 450 rooms, all with mahogany moldings and telephones. Half of them had private baths. This postcard billed it as "the world's largest, completely and continuously air-conditioned hotel." Located next to the beautiful Travis Park, it recognized the growing automobile trade by including a garage. (James Collett.)

For autocampers, San Antonio provided two tourist camps. One was in Brackenridge Park, seen here in the 1920s. Situated on the San Antonio River in one of the most beautiful parks in the country, campers enjoyed the peaceful feel of the countryside, only moments from downtown along Broadway Street. For those needing replacements, C.M. Swift on South Flores Street had camp outfits and tents for sale. (UTSA Special Collections.)

Grande Courts, attractively shown in this panoramic postcard, opened in 1923 and heralded the future of automobile-based lodging. Among the more elegant motor courts, Grande Courts provided both hotel comfort (private lodging, baths, sometimes even a kitchen) with the privacy of camping (separate cabins), as well as lodging for the motor car itself in the form of a garage, often with an additional private entrance to the cabin. (James Collett.)

Located further from downtown on Broadway, the San Antonio Park Mo-Tel offered a more compact, no-frills stay than Grande Courts. However, it also pointed to the future. Variations of these cottage courts and motor courts produced the motor hotel—the motel—that came into its own after World War II. As they continued their westward journey, OST travelers would encounter more examples of this developing form of lodging. (James Collett.)

Four

THROUGH THE HILL COUNTRY

On its 1917 map, the Texas Highway Department drew Highway 3 west from San Antonio to Del Rio, with Highways 12 and 17 continuing the road to Fort Stockton, then along Highway 10 to El Paso. The Old Spanish Trail Organization, however, carved a different path, a diagonal road rambling through the Texas Hill Country from San Antonio to Ozona. The 1925 West Texas edition *Travelog* made the case for "leaving the monotony of driving hour after hour beside a railroad track." The mileage would be shorter, and the country would be more inviting. This was "spring-water country," with over a dozen clear-water rivers, and rugged hills and mountains providing constantly changing scenes. Though all true, it glossed over the challenges of "interesting" driving over miles and miles of gravel, caliche, and dirt roads, constantly climbing up steep grades and then braking through a series of switchback curves. In the eastern segment, the highway often followed rivers (like the Guadalupe or the Llano) for miles, crossing them multiple times. By the time drivers reached Sonora and Ozona, the canyons held dry creeks, which could quickly turn to deadly floods after heavy rains.

Towns grew fewer as farming gave way to ranching—cattle, sheep, and goats. Kerrville was the only city between San Antonio and El Paso with more than 4,000 people. Distances between services—food, gasoline, lodging—increased. Yet, as the *Travelog* pointed out, "The people are hospitable and make the traveler feel welcome." The energetic and dedicated campaigns of several West Texas communities—Comfort, Junction, Sonora, and further west, Fort Stockton—to bring the trail down their main streets helped the OST leaders develop a path across this challenging landscape. The newly minted transcontinental route transformed these isolated rural hamlets into essential stops for travelers and places where they might take the time to enjoy the beauty of the Texas Hill Country.

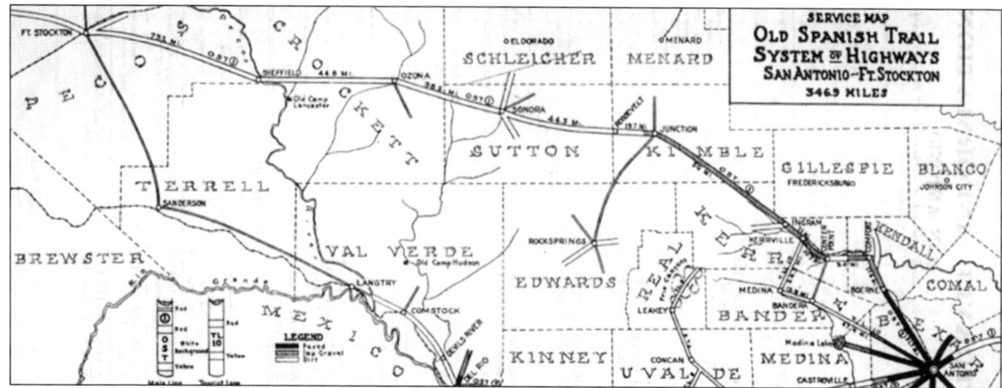

The first 50 miles of the 1920s road west from San Antonio was paved. The rest of the Hill Country route quickly became more challenging. This 1923 map segment indicated that over 100 miles were dirt, and the rest were classified as "improved gravel." The straight-line segments indicating mileage between communities provided no sense of actual road patterns winding through the central Texas hills. (Old Spanish Trail Centennial Celebration Association.)

The OST route (seen here near Comfort) followed the natural contours of the landscape, with little cutting or leveling, creating a rippling rising and falling of the highway, which taxed automobile engines. The 1925 *Travelog* promised a drive "through green valleys and along clear water streams, with a new picture at every turn of the road," a picturesque description for winding climbs, steep descents, and frequent river crossings. (UTSA Special Collections.)

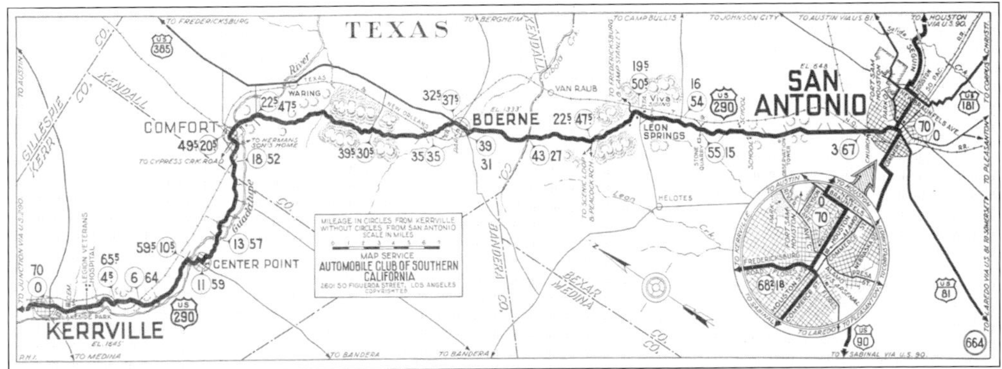

The strip maps of the 1933 Automobile Club of Southern California's *Guide to the Old Spanish Trail Highway* captured the highway's path in far greater detail. Curves, river crossings, connecting roads, passages through hilly terrain, and frequent mileage points provided motorists with a more realistic plan of daily travel. Additional information—county boundaries, park locations, and scenic attractions—would also become regular features on folding maps. (James Collett.)

As Hill Country tourism grew, the region developed many attractions to tempt travelers not fully dedicated to logging miles to linger. The region's limestone formations contained several natural caverns that developed into commercial ventures. A short 10 miles northeast of Boerne, the Cave Without A Name opened in 1939. Visitors wandered through six rooms at a constant 66 degrees filled with a spectacular array of speleothems. (James Collett.)

Comfort billed itself as "the Gateway to the Guadalupe Hills." Kendall County sent several delegates to the 1919 OST convention. Community leaders quickly realized the economic potential. By 1922, plans were underway to create a tourist campsite at the Comfort Guadalupe River Bridge. The June 8, 1922, *Comfort News* remarked on the growing automobile traffic, proposing, "Let's accept them cheerfully, and then prepare to profit by them." (Comfort Heritage Foundation.)

By 1925, Comfort had a beautiful tourist camp on the Guadalupe River. The OST *Travelog* promised "country hotels, good meals." Those needing directions or assistance could seek out OST councilor William Wiedenfeld (seen here with his grandson Harold around 1914). Wiedenfeld, a cashier at the Comfort State Bank, attended the 1919 San Antonio OST convention and became an avid promoter for bringing the road to Comfort. (Comfort Heritage Foundation.)

The Comfort OST Filling Station stood across the street from the Comfort State Bank. The visible cylinder–style pump was developed in the mid-1920s. Comfort was established by German immigrants in 1854. Proprietor Robert Stahmann, himself a German immigrant, provided travelers a bit of international flair in this rural community. In addition to gasoline, Stahmann offered travelers a café, a confectionery, and a ladies' restroom. (Comfort Heritage Foundation.)

Dan T. Holekamp established Holekamp Motor Company on High Street around 1920, installing a large elevator for lifting vehicles to a second-story shop. Holekamp sold Chevrolet cars in the Comfort area (a 1924 Superior Roadster costing $490), adding a Buick inventory in 1924 (sign on the far right). Along with gasoline at curbside pumps, Holekamp provided travelers another liquid, serving as the Lone Star Beer Agency headquarters. (Comfort Heritage Foundation.)

Pat Faust purchased the renovated Doebbler Garage building on High Street in 1920 as the OST was being laid out. An unidentified group stands in the new facility, complete with a front display room, a machine shop in the back, and a new concrete floor throughout. The garage offered day and night service. A handwritten sign specifies that gasoline sales must be cash. (Comfort Heritage Foundation.)

Westbound OST travelers faced rugged roads that could wreak havoc with tires, brakes, and shocks. Those reaching Comfort from the west might often need repairs or replacements. This 1920 ad from the *Comfort News* encouraged the purchase of Goodyear Heavy Tourist Tubes. Clincher tires were difficult to remove and replace when they blew, so a good tube that properly reinforced the tire casing was a wise investment. (Comfort Heritage Foundation.)

In 1918, Magnolia Petroleum Company made Comfort a gasoline and oil storage point, constructing a warehouse and tank. G.H. D'Albini served as company agent. As longer-distance automobile travel increased, it became important to establish distribution points beyond urban areas. Here, a driver refuels at the Comfort Magnolia station. This portion of the OST route was designated US 290 Highway (see canopy column) in the late 1920s. (Comfort Heritage Foundation.)

West of Comfort, the OST followed the Guadalupe River to Kerrville, climbing into the heart of the Hill Country. Travelers were promised "dry, breeze-laden air, and interesting drives," In the 1920s, much of that drive contained frequent curves in loose gravel, caliche, or graded dirt, requiring motorists to pay close attention and allow the passengers to enjoy the beautiful vistas. (James Collett.)

In 1938, the W.M. Cline Company began publishing real-photo postcards of scenes across the nation. The labeling and code identify this as a Cline card. The limestone rock barrier along the highway edge blended well with the landscape but hardly disguised the fact it was designed to prevent a precipitous plummet into the steep Hill Country canyons, though the alternative might still be a bone-jarring stop. (James Collett.)

Approaching Kerrville, the Old Spanish Trail Highway entered Texas ranch country, bringing another unexpected hazard requiring quick reflexes and good brakes. The likelihood of encountering livestock on a Hill Country highway was common enough that it became a postcard subject. Livestock—in this case, sheep—might transfer pastures along the highway right-of-way. The 1925 *Travelog* described Kerrville as "the largest primary wool and mohair market in Texas." (James Collett.)

Prominent among Hill Country livestock was the Angora goat, dramatically posed in this E.C. Kropp postcard. Mohair, the long silky hair of the Angora, is among the most prized natural fibers used to create a wide variety of items, from high-end sweaters to carpets and upholstery. Most US mohair comes from Texas, primarily the West Texas Edwards Plateau region, the southernmost unit of the Great Plains. (James Collett.)

Kerrville of the 1920s was a growing, prosperous city that offered travelers many amenities, including two OST councilors, Ally Beitel and Hal Peterson. The Guadalupe River tourist camp had electric lights, flush toilets, city water, and showers. For those seeking elegance, the old St. Charles Hotel, remodeled from this Victorian look into a three-story stucco building, had 63 guest rooms and a dining room that could seat 125 guests. (James Collett.)

Kerrville grew rapidly in the 1920s, fueled by tourism to the Hill Country and growing OST traffic. In 1927, the new five-story (soon expanded to eight) Blue Bonnet Hotel opened downtown on Water Street. The 140-room facility rented business spaces on the ground floor. Guests had ready access to a soda fountain (note the Coca-Cola sign), a barbershop, a beauty parlor, a coffee shop, and a newsstand. (James Collett.)

During the Great Depression, the Farm Security Administration sent photographers onto the American roads to document life in rural communities. Russell Lee was among those assigned the Midwest. In Kerrville, he found an enterprising tire repair shop in an old streetcar. While hard times slowed tourism, they drove others out onto the highways as migrants seeking work who might need a cheaper tire-repair option. (Library of Congress.)

In 1935, US Highway 290 was rerouted north of Kerrville through Fredericksburg, and the highway to Junction became Texas Highway 27. Kerrville's Del Norte Tourist Courts offered kitchenettes, garages, and a café with "really fine food." A United Motor Courts sign was also prominently displayed. This referral chain, established in 1933 by independently owned motels, guaranteed overnight travelers a standard of quality and cleanliness by its members. (James Collett.)

West of Kerrville, drivers followed the Guadalupe River upstream along a gravel road to the small town of Ingram, where the 1925 *Travelog* commented, "Wild country west along the river." The OST continued up the Johnson Creek fork of the river to Mountain Home, with its tree-shaded mountain spring tourist camp overseen by councilor N.B. Estes, then over the divide and down to Junction on the Llano River. (James Collett.)

Telephone 51 and "Count the Minutes"

Travelers needing assistance on the rough Hill Country roads could count on Junction's Powell Motor Company, who advertised their speedy service on the front of their postcard. The back contained mileage tables giving OST distances east and west of Junction. In addition to fast tow service, the garage had Texaco gasoline, ice and water, and separate restrooms for ladies and gents. (James Collett.)

The 1920s OST route into Junction lay along Cedar Creek, crossing it several times before skirting the mountain below Lover's Leap, where the creek met the Llano River. Junction derived its name from its location at the joining of the North and South Llano "spring-water rivers." Just across the bridge, the public tourist camp was in a pecan grove on the riverbank near where the rivers met. (James Collett.)

The 1920s Llano River bridge contained a single truss with metal and wire safety railings. The star within a circle (right truss) identified State Highway 27. Wooden planking smoothed the crossing, giving drivers a scenic view of the Llano River valley. The 1925 *Travelog* commented, "Shade is abundant; the mountain formations are wild and rugged," adding, "There are 500 miles of spring-fed streams in [Kimble] county." (Kimble County Historical Museum.)

Community leaders such as Coke Stevenson, an OST association vice president, realized the economic benefits of a transcontinental highway through Junction. They worked diligently for the Hill Country route in the face of competing options and less-than-enthusiastic state government support. A series of concrete columns containing the OST signage proudly marked the highway down dusty 1924 Main Street. Junction Hardware (on the right) became "a good information headquarters." (Kimble County Historical Museum.)

In this 1920s image, the obelisk-shaped markers include decorative globe lights and traffic signal lights at a street-view level. The corner post (right) has a Texas State Highway 27 marker. Federal and state demarcations replaced OST signage. Loeffler Motor Company (left) had a fireproof garage and drive-in gasoline station. The 1925 *Travelog* encouraged travelers to seek OST councilor Emil Loeffler for "information of any sort." (Kimble County Historical Museum.)

Junction's embrace of the OST included frequent employment of the obelisks in community events, from serving as a maypole to being festooned with decorative banners for parades (as seen on the left). Businesses along Main Street made special efforts to welcome travelers. The Gann Grocery sign included parking instructions. The City Café advertised in OST literature that it had good meals at all hours and tourists' restrooms and washrooms. (Kimble County Historical Museum.)

Junction's Piggly Wiggly was part of a small 1920s chain operated by the C.C. Butt Company of Kerrville. Travelers seeking supplies appreciated the new store model. Instead of handing the grocer their list, shoppers selected the price-marked items from open shelves, loading them into another innovation, a shopping cart. The popularity of this shopping style allowed the Butt Company to create its own store chain, eventually named H-E-B. (Kimble County Historical Museum.)

Junction lodging included Price's Tourist Camp on the banks of the Llano. However, in June 1935, widespread heavy rains across Central Texas flooded several Texas rivers, disrupting travel. The Llano crested at 43 feet on June 14, covering the highway, washing away tourist cabins, submerging gasoline stations and homes, and eventually destroying the bridge over the river. A new larger bridge was completed in 1937. (Kimble County Historical Museum.)

Junction's Fritz Hotel offered safer, more elegant accommodations. Seen here in the 1920s, Fritz's advertising proclaimed it "a bit of new Spanish architecture on the Old Spanish Trail." A 1923 OST service map declared it the "best beds and meals on the Trail." Local Coke Stevenson, president of Junction's First National Bank and later governor of Texas, purchased the 37-room hotel in the 1930s, renaming it Las Lomas. (James Collett.)

As OST traffic grew, so did the lodging options in Junction. In the 1930s, the renovated Kimble Courts proclaimed, "We're on the Highway now!" This 30-unit tourist court included separate-unit apartments and hotel rooms, each with a private bath and circulating hot water from insulated underground lines, electric or gas stoves for cooking and heating, and a playground, all on a well-manicured five acres. The rates in 1936 were $1.50 to $4. (James Collett.)

In the 1930s, the Texas Highway Department provided work relief through road construction in response to growing auto-tourism and Texas centennial celebrations, paving roads, straightening routes, and improving grades and drainages, all part of state engineer Gibb Gilchrist's effort to make the highway department a professional organization. The road into Kerrville was carved down Lover's Leap to the 1,342-foot-long blacktop-paved 1937 bridge. (Kimble County Historical Museum.)

The finished road descended in sinuous curves into Junction, giving travelers a panoramic view of the city and the North Llano River. After 1930, Texas highways had wider right-of-ways containing no commercial advertising. This 1949 Curt Teich postcard utilized a photograph from the studio of Junction photographer James Murff. New Deal photographer Russell Lee captured this same view earlier in 1939, as seen on the cover. (Kimble County Historical Museum.)

Among the most colorful travelers the OST brought to Junction was Walter Wonderwell, arriving in 1929 with his unique vehicle, his young wife, translator, driver, and filmmaker Aloha, "the world's most widely traveled girl," and her pet monkey Chango. Wanderwell claimed to be the first to drive a car around the world, covering 175,000 miles. Souvenirs of his journey and a Dunlop Tyres advertisement cover the car. (Kimble County Historical Museum.)

Departing Junction, drivers forded the North Llano River several times before later bridge construction. They were warned to change to a lower gear and "go across steadily." On the plateau after Fort Terrett, they faced another challenge of ranch country: bumper gates, as seen here. Those failing to properly change gears and "push through quickly" carried reminders in scraped doors and dented bumpers. (Texas Department of Transportation.)

Navigating bumper gate country, travelers might encounter shearing crews. By the 1920s, Texas ranchers raised two million Angora goats, producing over 80 percent of the American mohair clip. Angora goats were sheared twice yearly, in the spring before kidding and in fall prior to breeding season. Mexican nationals made up many of the crews. Here, a shearing crew rests on the Edward Sawyer Ft. Terrett Ranch. (Sutton County Historical Society.)

In the years of almost nonexistent highway signage, the *Automobile Blue Book* provided travelers with detailed assistance. This 1927 edition described the road between San Antonio and Ozona, elaborating road conditions (pavement, gravel, stone, and dirt), comments on the landscape (very pretty country), and specific turn-by-turn directions using local landmarks (at the courthouse, lumber yard, printing office) along the 229-mile route. Trips were listed twice—once in each direction. (James Collett.)

Hiway No.	Mileage	
27	58.9	CENTER POINT, end of road. Right.
27	70.0	KERRVILLE.
27	71.1	End of road; right.
27	77.5	INGRAM, right-hand road. Right.
27	89.2	EURA. Cross Llano River 126.4.
27	126.9	JUNCTION.
27	127.2	End of road; right.
27	127.4	End of road; left.
27	127.8	End of road; right.
27	132.7	Prom. fork; left thru ford.
27	147.0	ROOSEVELT. Follow travel along Llano River, crossing same numerous times.
27	185.8	Left-hand road; left.
27	191.4	4-cor. at courthouse; right, then left 1 blk.
27	191.5	SONORA, 4-cor. at printing office. Right 1 blk., then left 1 blk.
27	191.6	4-cor. at lumber yard; right.
27	191.7	Fork at ball park; right.
27	191.9	Fork at three roads at windmill; keep middle road.
27	201.2	Fork beyond gate; left.
27	229.6	OZONA, 4-cor. at far side of park. Left is Route 594 to Ft. Stockton.

Route 592R—Ozona to Junction and San Antonio, Tex.—229.6 m.

Pavement, gravel, stone and dirt. A section of the Old Spanish Trail.

This route traverses a very pretty country and exceptionally good camping sites are to be found along the numerous creeks and streams.

Hiway No.	Mileage	
	0.0	OZONA, at southwest corner of park. Go east, passing courthouse on left.
27	7.1	Fork; right.
27	27.4	Prom. fork; right.
27	38.0	4-cor. at lumber yard; left 1 blk., then right 1 blk.
27	38.1	SONORA, 4-cor. at printing office. Left.
27	38.2	End of street at courthouse; right and immediately left. Left at 43.8 leads to Menard. From mileage 72.2 to Junction the road follows general course of Llano River.
27	82.7	ROOSEVELT. Cross Llano River 100.9.
27	101.8	Left-hand road; left.
27	102.2	Right-hand road; right.
27	102.4	Left-hand road; left onto Main St.
27	102.7	JUNCTION. Cross Llano River 103.2.
27	140.4	EURA.
27	152.1	INGRAM, end of road. Left.
27	158.5	Left-hand road; left.
27	159.6	KERRVILLE.
27	170.5	CENTER POINT. Keep ahead.
27	170.7	Left-hand road; left.
27	178.1	Right-hand road; right.
27	179.9	Right-hand road at RR; right.
27	180.2	COMFORT.
27	190.3	Right-hand road; right.
9	197.9	BOERNE.
9	198.6	Left-hand road at store; left.
9	207.1	Left-hand road; left.
9	210.1	End of road at RR; right.
9	210.2	LEON SPRINGS. San Antonio City Map and Pts. of Int., Route 520.
9	229.1	Houston St.; left.
9	229.6	SAN ANTONIO, Houston & Alamo Sts., at Alamo Square. HOTELS: Gunter, Menger. No left turns can be made on Houston or Commerce Sts. between Flores and Alamo Sts. Left is Route 520 (Highway 2) to Austin; ahead is Route 583 (Highway 3) to Houston; right is Route 605 (Highway 16) to Corpus Christi.

Route 594—Ozona to Fort Stockton, Tex.—117.5 m.

Natural gravel and dirt. A section of the Old Spanish Trail.

Traverses plateaus and broken prairie country, with but few signs of habitation. Cattle raising is the main industry. Fine camping sites are found along the wooded shores of Live Oak Creek, 10 miles east of Sheffield.

Hiway No.	Mileage	
	0.0	OZONA, at courthouse. South.
	0.3	4-cor. at ball park; right and follow main highway. Cross Pecos River 41.2.
27	44.7	SHEFFIELD, end of road. Left.
27	44.9	Irreg. 4-cor.; square right.
27	77.2	Fork; left.
27	113.1	End of road; left, and next right.
27	117.1	Diag. 4-cor.; left. Sharp right across RR is Route 595 (Highway 27) to Sierra Blanca.
27	117.5	FORT STOCKTON, at bank.

The 1925 OST councilors Joe Trainer and W.L. Aldwell, Sonora's First National Bank president, served Sonora travelers. Trainer co-owned the Vanderstucken-Trainer General Store and is shown here with an employee answering the phone. The 1920s road into Sonora was "under construction along a scenic ridge." The 1925 *Travelog* suggested "stops and better acquaintance with the people of West Texas are worthwhile," perhaps while auto repairs were underway. (Sutton County Historical Society.)

In the 1929 *Travelog*, Sonora Motor Company owner S.R. Hull advertised 14,500 feet of floor space, a large tire stock, modern repair equipment, and day and night Lone Star service. C.S. Keene's City Garage, also well-equipped, had a mechanic and free ice water. In addition, Sonora had the Dew Drop Inn, with cigars and tourists' restroom, and even a McDonald's—Josie McDonald's hotel. (Sutton County Historical Society.)

Rough road conditions west from Junction made knowledge of good garages (such as this one in Sonora) and their hours of service critical for long-distance travelers. OST *Travelogs* regularly listed them, often with recommendations. Sonora's City Garage had "good mechanics." Ozona's Dudley Garage was fireproof and the "largest between San Antonio and El Paso." Sheffield had Hale's Garage, described as "good for so small a settlement." (Sutton County Historical Society.)

The Sonora to Ozona road was 38 miles of gravel and dirt. Ozona's tourist camp included a screened dining room, shower baths, toilets, electric lights, and even wood. OST councilor Joe Oberkampf's furniture and hardware store, next door to the Ozona National Bank, had cooking and camping goods for travelers seeking to resupply. The Ozona Hotel, built in 1893, provided "old, good meals." (James Collett.)

You Can Build a Charming Home Yet Keep the Cost Low

For tourists seeking Western fare, R.J. Cooke's Ozona Meat Market had the "finest barbecue meat," with day and night service. A 1927 ad in the *Ozona Stockman* (also owned by Cooke) indicted that the meat market also offered bologna and oysters. Before leaving Ozona for the "famed country West of the Pecos," travelers were encouraged to stock up with supplies and the good drinking water. (Portal to Texas History.)

This 1939 large-letter postcard placed Sonora and Ozona within West Texas, though they also retained Hill Country attributes. Large-letter cards filled each blocky letter with illustrations of a city, state, or, in this case, region. Western and historic themes dominate, though the "X" recognizes in dramatic fashion the development of the Permian Basin oil fields. The message is, "This is the Wild West!" (James Collett.)

Five

LONG TREK ACROSS WEST TEXAS

West of Ozona lay the challenging Trans-Pecos terrain. Steep-sloped, sparsely vegetated, limestone-capped mesas replaced rounded hills and live oaks. The topography allowed for durable, though often unforgiving, roads. Following his 1925 journey there, Harral Ayres remarked, "Fast time is made but the driver takes risks." That same year, travelers negotiated 300 miles of gravel and dirt road before again reaching pavement. Into the 1930s, over 100 miles remained "scheduled for construction."

At the Pecos River, the OST joined the path of the San Antonio–San Diego Mail Line, established in the 1850s, and generally followed it west to El Paso. Leaving Sheffield, the highway followed Four-Mile Draw, crossing the divide to Bakersfield. Low mesas and isolated buttes became common as drivers crossed a corner of the giant West Texas oil fields. The country became open land around Fort Stockton, with its Comanche Springs oasis. Heading west into a realm of sand, distance, and mountains, travelers were warned, "Stock up carefully." Passing the Davis Mountains, formed by volcanic activity, they reached a second oasis at Balmorhea, with beautiful side trips available into Limpia Canyon. At Scroggins Draw, the OST merged with the Bankhead, US Highway 80. The road traversed mountain ranges—the Apache, Delaware, and Guadalupe—then crossed the desert terrain of Salt Flats. On clear days, drivers might glimpse Guadalupe Peak, the highest point in Texas.

Past Van Horn and Sierra Blanca, named for the nearby towering volcanic cone, the road descended into the Rio Grande drainage, sandy dunes, and the Franklin Mountains rising in the west. Weary travelers followed the tree-shaded valley road past Ysleta Mission into El Paso, the final major Texas city. Some took time for a short jaunt across to Juarez, Mexico. Finally, the OST wound around the Franklin Mountains to Anthony and into New Mexico. Those pausing for a photograph at the state border who consulted their maps happily realized they were closer to San Diego than to the eastern border of Texas. If they reflected on the long miles, they realized the Texas OST had been a memorable odyssey.

Twenty-eight miles west of Ozona, the road sharply descended the Edwards Plateau to Live Oak Creek, joining the route blazed by the San Antonio–San Diego Mail Line to California. With few deviations, the first OST route closely followed this line across the remainder of Texas. Drivers could only imagine riding a stage down the steep grade. (Old Spanish Trail Association Archives, St. Mary's University.)

Live Oak Creek featured drinkable water and large oak groves. The ruins of Fort Lancaster, active in the 1850s, lay near the mouth of the creek. Wall and chimney portions remained, though many of the limestone blocks became local construction material. Travelers like Bernard Carr (photographed in 1933 by Joe Christian from Eldorado, Texas) stopped to wander the ruins and imagine life on the rough Texas frontier. (Texas Historical Commission.)

In the 1930s, the Texas Highway Department undertook various projects to straighten and improve segments of the OST route. Among these was constructing a new descent to Live Oak Creek at a point above Old Fort Lancaster. A curving path with protective rock walls was carved along the side of a shallow canyon across from where the stage road once descended precariously to the historic post. (Texas Department of Transportation.)

The work produced a scenic two-mile descent providing dramatic vistas of the Pecos River valley. A roadside park containing concrete dining tables and fireplaces beneath stone and concrete arbors was later constructed at the top of Lancaster Hill. During the Great Depression, the National Youth Administration built roadside parks across Texas in a beautification and safety program under the direction of state highway engineer Gib Gilchrist. (James Collett.)

The Pecos River Bridge near Sheffield marked the last river westbound OST travelers would cross in Texas, though numerous dry arroyos and draws lay ahead. In the early 1900s, Sheffield resident Ed Miller proudly drove Sheffield's first car over the bridge. Accompanying him were Eunice Miller (left), Maggie Taylor, and two passengers in back. In 1934 (see page 125), a new bridge was erected a few miles downriver. (Wayne Holmes.)

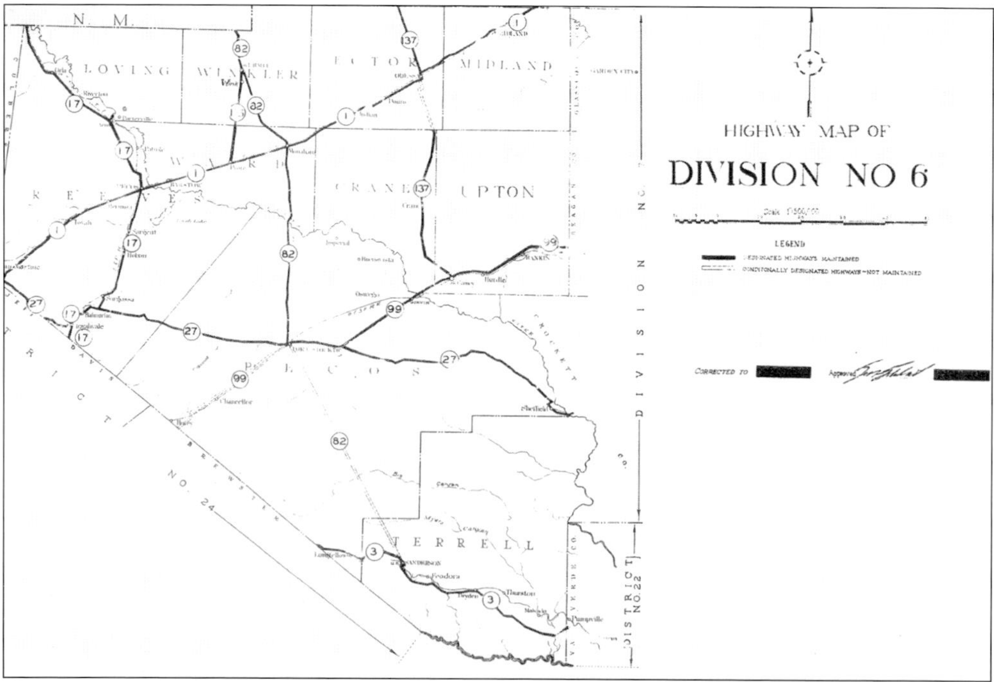

Pecos County was crucial to the OST West Texas route Harral Ayres preferred. Aware of construction along a competitive Del Rio route, he pushed Pecos County officials to improve their OST portion. Recognizing the commercial significance, Fort Stockton leaders responded, though not always as rapidly as Ayres wished. This 1920s highway division map shows Pecos County's 110 OST miles—more than any other Texas county. (Nita Stewart Haley Memorial Library.)

Fort Stockton was active in the early 1900s Good Roads Movement, constructing many miles of roads. Years later, Ayres found them in decay, reporting the Pecos County OST as "a fair road, but not a good road" with "ancient concrete dips" that damaged shocks and frames. To help early travelers, some unknown worker neatly incised a good-luck swastika into the concrete of a Pecos County culvert, which is still intact. Before the 1930s, the swastika was an ancient and popular good-luck symbol, appearing as an architectural motif and in advertising, including for Coca-Cola. (Warren Nutt.)

Sheffield's dusty street offered the chance for a brief break from miles of washboard dirt road, bumper gates, and concrete-paved arroyo crossings. The two garages offered all-night service and promised that mechanics C.E. Hale and Jerome Lackey could handle all repairs. Ellington's ranch supply store wanted tourists to know there were also supplies for them. The 1925 *Travelog* warned that "long miles without houses" lay ahead. (Wayne Holmes.)

One intrepid family recorded their journey across the empty spaces of the West Texas OST in a series of long-faded photographs. The same three children appear in several of them. Perhaps the one that best captures the adventurous spirit of crossing "the big cattle country" in those years is this one taken somewhere in arid western Texas and simply labeled, "Where we waited while they paved the road." (James Collett.)

Another 1920s traveler stopped for a photograph near Bakersfield, beneath the pyramid-shaped peak in the background. Without a caption, the driver's unusual pose is indecipherable, but the photograph captures the harsh climate, wide horizons, and sense of isolation travelers from other regions must have felt. The Fox-Tone image was printed by the Fox Company of San Antonio, the world's largest photofinishing business in the 1920s. (James Collett.)

In the 1930s, Highway 290 was paved in the vicinity of Bakersfield (background, right of center). The small community was established in 1929 after the discovery of the Taylor-Link oil field, dwindling after a short boom. The oil field remained; ground-level flares were a common feature. Night drivers found themselves passing through the spectacle of bright orange flames glowing like abandoned bonfires through the mesquite brush. (Texas Department of Transportation.)

Fort Stockton quickly faced a problem eventually affecting many OST communities. Rather than passing through the original business district, the road followed the Orient Railroad along the northern edge of town, then west down Tenth Street. A mile east of town, an alternate street led to downtown. Dueling billboards invited travelers to consider which OST to take—to the "Heart of Fort Stockton" or Highway 27. (Texas Department of Transportation.)

In this pre-franchise era, businesses sought to attract highway travelers by adding the OST initials to their operations. While actually denoting no official licensing by the OST organization, the name might provide an extra degree of trust when choosing fuel, food, auto repairs, or lodging. This billboard for an enterprising Fort Stockton business offering all four options made certain that tourists got the message. (Texas Department of Transportation.)

Fort Stockton's early businesses developed near Comanche Springs. In this view from atop the Pecos County Courthouse, the springs are right of center. The historic Riggs Hotel is at lower right. Main Street runs north from the courthouse, past Rooney Mercantile. Two roads come from the right (east), converging at First Street to bring OST traffic past the Alamo Filling Station to downtown Fort Stockton. (Fort Stockton Historical Society.)

The Alamo Filling Station (seen here in 1927) bore no resemblance to the famous structure. Like countless other businesses appropriating the name over the years, the little station hoped it might persuade the traveler to choose it. Its billboard (see page 89) utilized the famous Texian battle cry in its advertising and even reproduced the interesting "accent" marks seen here in the station's signage. (Fort Stockton Historical Society.)

The view from beneath the Alamo's canopy was the perspective of hundreds of Texans in the chain of towns strung along the OST. Often living in small, rural communities, they became linked to the cosmopolitan stream of people flowing through town. Neighboring Texans, drivers from far-flung states, and even infrequent international travelers represented income and a brief connection with the world beyond their dusty street. (Fort Stockton Historical Society.)

Fort Stockton locals also took OST journeys, both long and short. Agnes Butz (center), wife of entrepreneur Herman H. Butz, and children (from left to right) Walter, Karl, and Marvin, accompanied by Emma Butz, are dressed for travel, perhaps to Herman's hometown of New Braunfels. Luggage was strapped to running boards to provide room for everyone. The fresh-dressed look quickly wilted over the long, hot, dusty miles. (Fort Stockton Historical Society.)

Though Rooney Mercantile had operated for many years, founder James Rooney supported the OST's arrival, becoming a councilor. The "complete department store" occupied several thousand square feet, containing a variety of goods including camp and auto supplies. Rooney Mercantile employees included, from left to right, Lupe Terrazas (delivery truck driver), Pilar Duran, Velma James, Doug Adams, E.O. Gonzales, Cleve Nunn, and R.H. Hughes. (Courtesy of the Joe Primera family.)

By the 1930s, businesses spread along the Highway 290 path through Fort Stockton, but Main Street remained a vibrant area. State Highway 82 ran down Main Street (markers on utility poles). Across First Street from Rooney Mercantile (to the right of the photograph) was the two-story New Rooney Hotel, which included a café. Next door on Main Street was the Pouncey Grocery. Young's Café was across the street. (Fort Stockton Historical Society.)

The Hotel Stockton, built in 1911 near the tracks of the Orient Railroad, which arrived in Fort Stockton the following year, benefitted from being close to the new Highway 290 route along Tenth Street. The 1925 OST *Travelog* billed it as the "largest, best-equipped hotel between San Antonio and El Paso." The establishment had 70 rooms, steam heating, a dining room, and a vast ballroom. (Pecos County Historical Commission.)

Among the businesses along Fort Stockton's OST was the Gateway Lodge, built in the 1930s–1940s motor court style and included in the Texas Department of Health "List of Texas Courts and Lodges" booklet in 1940. Its 17 units were steam heated, double-bed kitchenettes with private bathrooms and attached garages. The 1941 Duncan Hines lodging guide stated, though exteriors were "not especially attractive," the rooms offered "clean and comfortable restfulness." (James Collett.)

Fort Stockton offered travelers a special surprise: its Comanche Springs oasis. The springs had always provided the water critical to the city's existence and been a site for social gatherings, from baptisms to picnics. OST travelers and locals such as these could enjoy a refreshing dip in the large spring-fed pool. The 1925 tourist camp included electric lights, dressing rooms, and access to the swimming pool. (Fort Stockton Historical Society.)

94

During the Depression years, Fort Stockton obtained Works Progress Administration funds for a major revision of the pool (underway in this 1937 postcard). A new bathhouse and concrete steps were added, along with an improved road beside the two spring outlets. Beginning in 1936, the city held a Water Carnival beauty pageant and swimming and diving show at the pool, which became an annual event. (Fort Stockton Historical Society.)

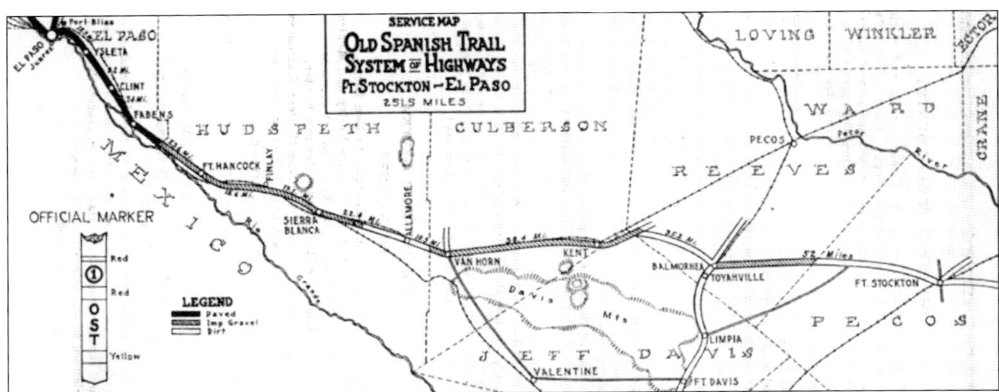

As it had throughout Texas, the OST west of Fort Stockton offered travelers more dramatically different terrain. Drivers entered a forbidding desert land containing stark mountain ranges and extreme weather. Blistering hot in summer, dangerous icy storms swept down during the winter months. Most of the road was paved by the 1930s, but the 1920s were a different story—over 200 miles of dirt and gravel. (OST100 *Travelog* collection.)

After winding through a 12-mile valley of irrigated farms, the OST reached Balmorhea, another spring-fed desert oasis. In 1934, Civilian Conservation Corps (CCC) Company 186 began construction of a state park at San Solomon Springs four miles west of Balmorhea. Seen here in 1938, the project included a barracks, mess hall, and kitchen serving 200 young men and supervisors. Building materials were local limestone and adobe bricks. (Texas Parks and Wildlife.)

Balmorhea State Park, which opened in 1940, included a 1.3-acre double-wing pool around the springs, a concession building, two bathhouses, and the San Solomon Courts—red-tile-roofed white plaster adobe brick cabins with garages. Highway 290, the OST (seen here) ran beside the new park, enticing tourists to stop. It also became a gateway to the Davis Mountains, along State Highway 17 just west of the pool. (Texas Parks and Wildlife.)

In the 1930s, travelers encountered another adventure at Balmorhea. Over 3,900 men and 4,000 horses from the 1st Cavalry, stationed at Fort Bliss, camped across State Highway 17 from the spring, conducting maneuvers. They were among the first to enjoy the newly built park. Fortunate tourists watched cavalry drills, recalling days of an earlier army in the west. In this 1938 press photograph, note the machine guns on the horses. (James Collett.)

For those with time, a detour south on State Highway 17 from Balmorhea into the Davis Mountains, a sky island (an isolated mountain range surrounded by desert), beckoned. Davis Mountains State Park was created in 1933 with 560 acres largely donated by landowners devastated by the Great Depression. The drive south curved through Limpia Canyon (seen here) and over scenic Wild Rose Pass with several pleasant picnic spots. (James Collett.)

The CCC constructed Davis Mountain State Park between 1933 and 1935, including Indian Lodge, seen here. The original 16-room pueblo-style hotel in scenic Keesey Canyon was built of hand-hewn pine beams and adobe blocks molded onsite. Rooms had longleaf pine floors, cane and log ceilings, hand-carved cedar furniture, and a plaza-like exterior courtyard, recalling Native American and Spanish architecture of the Southwest. (James Collett.)

On the way to Davis Mountains State Park, travelers passed the ruins of Fort Davis, perhaps stopping for a look at this piece of the Old West. Established in 1854, the post eventually closed in 1891. After its abandonment, civilians lived in the quarters. In the 1930s, as seen in this postcard, D.A. Simmons purchased the site and worked to preserve and maintain it in reasonable condition. (James Collett.)

The OST met the Bankhead Highway and Texas & Pacific Railroad at McElroy Junction, its designation becoming US Highway 80. Forty-nine miles later, the road ran down Broadway Street in Van Horn (seen here in the 1930s), a wide dusty street with mountains and desert terrain in the background, like something from a Western movie, but horses, buggies, and stage lines were replaced with gas stations, cafes, and tourist courts. (Clark Hotel Museum.)

In 1920, Fred Clark converted Van Horn's oldest building, an adobe saloon and post office erected around 1901, into the Clark Hotel, which quickly became a community hub. As the Bankhead and the OST brought highway traffic through Van Horn, more hotels and cafés joined the Clark along Broadway Street. In this 1920s photograph, the Clark and Jacksons have cafes, and a drugstore adjoins the Clark. (Clark Hotel Museum.)

Toolen's Tourist Camp, Van Horn, Texas. Steam Heated Rooms, Linens Furnished, Garages in Connection

Charlie Toolen built his tourist camp on the northeast side of Van Horn in 1915, while the OST and Bankhead were still more ideas than reality. With its surrounding wall, connected units, adjacent garages, planted trees, and associated filling station, Toolen's had a rudimentary Camp Grande look and perhaps better fit the court model. The entrance arch promised rates of $1 to $2. (James Collett.)

After the road was paved (see page 88), the anonymous family continued their journey west, stopping for the night at Toolen's Camp. This photograph reveals the camp's unfinished nature. The roughly plastered bare tiles have a haphazard design in places. There is a lack of any exterior steps or sidewalks, and the stake driven in the ground appears to indicate unfinished work. Perhaps the rooms were better. (James Collett.)

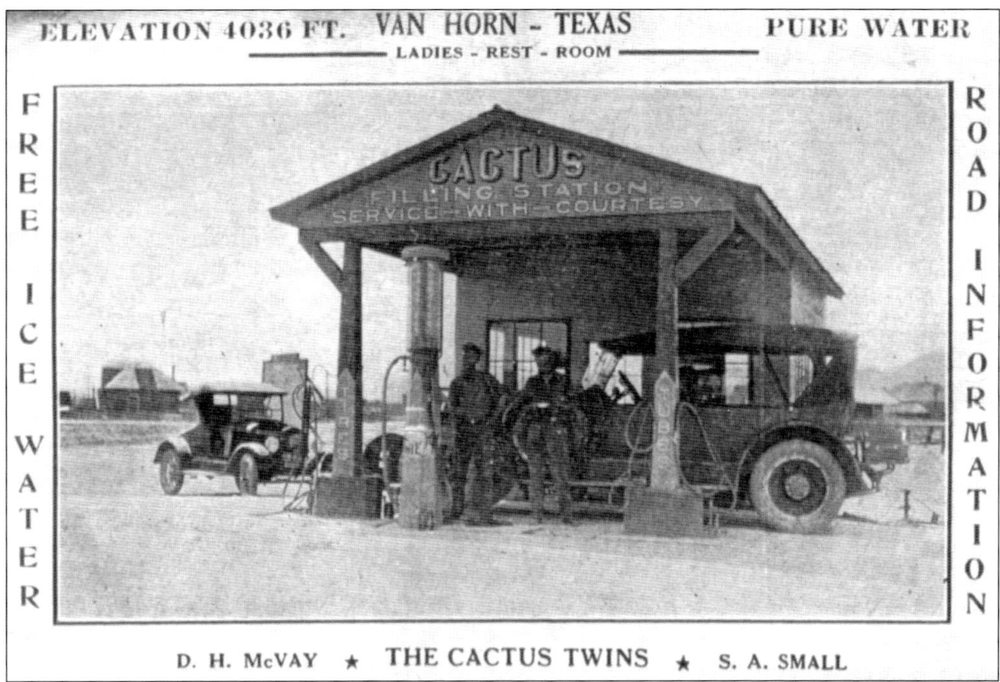

D. H. McVAY ★ THE CACTUS TWINS ★ S. A. SMALL

The "Cactus Twins," D.H. McVay and S.A. Small, were early Van Horn entrepreneurs. Their Cactus Filling Station, a basic box with canopy structure near the train depot, had a single visible-cylinder pump and no brand information. Miles from major cities, they recognized drivers' potential need of tires and tubes. McVay later incorporated the front of his station in his tourist courts on Broadway. (Clark Hotel Museum.)

Built in 1930, Van Horn's El Capitan was one of five Gateway hotels designed by famed architect Henry Trost. The 60-room hotel sat at the crossroads to three proposed national parks—Carlsbad Caverns, Guadalupe, and Big Bend. European tile lined the lobby floor, leading to stairwells with wrought-iron banisters. The 14-foot ceiling was made of exposed vigas. Room rates in 1941 began at $3. (James Collett.)

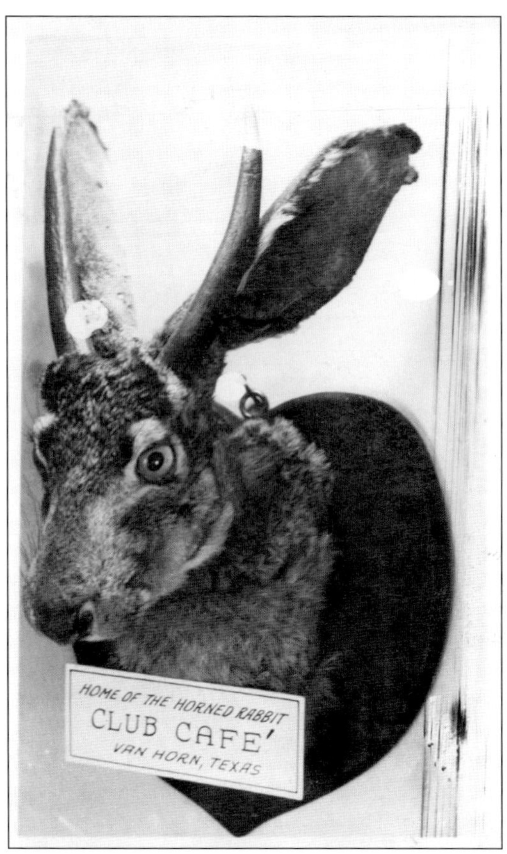

Van Horn's Club Café (as seen on page 99, right of the El Capitan) offered travelers an exotic animal, a rabbit with horns, a variant of the mythical jackalope, first popularized by taxidermists in the 1930s. Locals along transcontinental routes often manufactured creatures or tales to perplex or entertain those passing through. That bit of humor or wonder might help to bring in a bit of return or word-of-mouth trade. (James Collett.)

Sierra Blanca, beside an immense volcanic peak, marked the completion spot for the second transcontinental railroad in 1881 with the joining of the Texas & Pacific and Southern Pacific lines. The 1930s OST route turned El Paso Street into a bustling collection of travel-related roadside businesses by the 1940s. Those stopping learned that the town was split between the Central and Mountain time zones. (James Collett.)

The Owl Courts and Coffee Shop, with 1930s Art Deco styling and trim, billed itself as "modern." It also promised room service and locked garages as an additional security feature. Eva and George were possibly the owners, though this undated postcard provided no further details. The 1940 state guide of approved Texas courts and organized camps included the Sierra Blanca Owl Courts, listing H.E. Carpenter as owner. (James Collett.)

Sierra Blanca's "delux" El Patio Courts, also with closed garages, received a listing in the 1940 state guide. Duncan Hines also included it in his 1940 *Lodging For a Night* travel guide, compiled to help tourists consistently find acceptable, comfortable lodging. Hines said of El Patio, "The unusual fact is that here, miles away from everything, is a very good court." Rooms were $2.50, and pets were allowed. (James Collett.)

Like Van Horn's Club Café (see page 102), the Best Café of Sierra Blanca hoped its gimmick title might entice customers stopping in to later claim they dined there. This postcard made the claim that the café "lives up to its name by serving excellent foods at modern prices . . . in the Western manner." The Owl Courts across the street might have disagreed over who was Sierra Blanca's best. (James Collett.)

The 1920s OST followed the railroad from Sierra Blanca in an arid 35-mile northern arc before returning south to meet the Rio Grande at Fort Hancock (the 1930s redesign followed a more direct path west). The 60-mile tree-shaded Valley Road followed the Rio Grande into El Paso, through irrigation systems reaching back to Spanish times, fields, truck farms, and gardens, providing travelers a refreshing change. (James Collett.)

The Tigua Indians built the Corpus Christi de la Ysleta mission in 1682 in their Ysleta del Sur Pueblo, making it the oldest continuously operated parish in Texas. Over the years, storms and natural disasters damaged the adobe structure, but the Tigua always rebuilt. OST travelers could stop to visit the church, rebuilt after a disastrous 1907 fire with a restored bell tower and Spanish statue of Christ, which survived. (James Collett.)

El Paso, in far West Texas, was international, cosmopolitan, and historic, linking Mexico with the Southwest for centuries. The 1920s streetcar system included routes from downtown to Fort Bliss, Juarez, and Ysleta. On the right are the White House Department Store and Hotel, a Henry Trost Chicago commercial-style building. The basement and first floor held the department store, and the hotel occupied the remaining six stories. (James Collett.)

International Bridge between El Paso, Tex. and Juarez, Mex. — Juarez in the distance.

Exotic Juarez, Mexico, lay a short drive or trolley ride across the Rio Grande, with its marketplace, curio shops, and Plaza de Toros. The 1925 OST *Travelog* recommended Jimmie O'Brien's Downtown Café or Joe Mogel's Riverside Café. In the 1920s Prohibition era, visitors could also enjoy legal alcohol at cafes or cabarets. In these simpler times, passports were readily available from the El Paso Chamber of Commerce. (James Collett.)

The Hotel Paso Del Norte was unparalleled for those seeking a final, luxurious stay in Texas. The 10-story Henry Trost $1.5 million building (constructed in 1912) featured a 25-foot-diameter Tiffany-style glass dome in the lobby. Duncan Hines recommended its Mexican food. There was also the historic Hotel Sheldon, a meeting place for Mexican revolutionaries. When it burned in 1929, a new Hilton was constructed on the site. (James Collett.)

By the 1930s, El Paso had 33 tourist camps. Camp Grande, the largest, billed itself as the Southwest's premier camp, with accommodations for all needs—tents, cabins, cottages, community kitchens and laundries, baths, a recreation hall, restaurant, and a service station and garage with experienced mechanics. In this postcard, a shopping center, including a café and drugstore, lines both sides of the camp entrance. (James Collett.)

Located on Alameda Avenue on the OST, Camp Grande's entrance arch included a large swastika in its décor. By the late 1930s, Camp Grande had removed it. (James Collett.)

The Del Camino Courts at 4910 East Alameda Avenue earned listings in both the United Motor Courts and Duncan Hines 1941 guides, a definite advantage in the city's competitive lodging market. Another advantage was that a streetcar line to downtown ended here. Frank and Anabelle Cooke welcomed guests to the 52-cottage facility with "inviting air-conditioned rooms" with and without kitchenettes, which ranged from $3 to $7. (James Collett.)

Red Mill Camp and Courts, El Paso, Texas on No. 80

In an era before standardized roadside lodging, owners could design creatively. In 1929, Jack McDonald opened Red Mill Camp and Courts "to the tired traveler." On east Alameda, at the entrance to El Paso's Washington Park, it had quite eclectic architecture. Duncan Hines's 1941 recommendation included the laconic comment, "Interesting rustic architecture." Resembling a large pueblo with an incongruous thunderbird-adorned windmill, a Mexican silhouette stood beside the front doors. (James Collett.)

The Red Mill's interior was equally eclectic, mixing hunting lodge elements, Spanish colonial furnishing, Native American rugs, and lampshades with Western photographs. Yet, the courts garnered recommendations from United Motor Courts, Duncan Hines, and the American Automobile Association (AAA). One guest, June, started her postcard from the Red Mill with the comment, "How's this for a snazzy place?" Perhaps it was a fitting choice for the OST's more adventurous travelers. (James Collett.)

The Hitchin' Post gasoline station also used Southwestern-style architecture with a stucco-covered exterior and protruding wooden beams. Though selling Texaco gasoline, the only product branding is the Fire Chief logo (introduced in 1932) on the gas pumps. The lack of a canopy was less of a problem with El Paso's average 10 inches of annual rain, but also meant no shelter from the desert sun. (James Collett.)

In the 1930s, autocamping, a 1920s jaunt, took a serious turn. Unemployed Americans took to the highways searching for work. Farm Security Administration photographer Dorothea Lange photographed this unidentified African American wife preparing breakfast on the outskirts of El Paso. The migrant hotel maid, cook, and laundress told Lange, "Do you suppose I'd be out on the highway cooking my steak if I had it good at home?" (Library of Congress.)

In 1937, Texas placed these state line markers facing oncoming traffic at every highway crossing. Cut from Amarillo stone and set in a base of rock native to the various regions (see page 18), they became favorite spots for photographs, like this one of soldiers in the 1940s. Texas-shaped stones marked the two ends of the OST in Texas, with 900 adventurous driving miles lying between them. (James Collett.)

Six

TRANSFORMING THE TRAIL

After the end of World War II, Americans took to the highways in record numbers, ready to regularly spend their pent-up energy and new prosperity on vacations and weekend jaunts. The growth of air-conditioning in vehicles and roadside establishments made the Old Spanish Trail Highway's warm southern climate appealing.

Texas OST miles had been paved and straightened, the grades improved, and state and federal highway signage added. New roadside state parks offered opportunities for rest and recreation. For long-haul interstate travelers, the OST provided an efficient, fairly direct path across the vast state. Those more leisure-inclined found it to be a route to much of the history, culture, and diverse landscapes of the Lone Star State, from piney woods to Hill Country canyons to the western desert mountains. Shiny new state and national parks lay readily accessible from the trail.

This river of travelers offered tremendous opportunities to those dwelling along the roadside. Mom-and-pop businesses built the nation's travel industry during these years. They operated a local service station in corporate uniforms. They fed hungry tourists in eating establishments of all sizes serving all cuisines. For lodging, they turned courts into motels or constructed new accommodations. These mom-and-pop motels provided "home away from home" lodging with a growing list of amenities from toiletries to air conditioning and television. Many had coffee shops and pools as added attractions. Neon signs glowed in the night in a variety of shapes and colors designed to entice weary travelers to choose this spot for one or more nights of rest.

As vacationers sought greater uniformity and advance knowledge about the quality of lodging, organizations arose to help guarantee standards of quality. Corporations, sensing economic opportunity, entered the market. Motel chains and fast-food franchises sprouted along the road, bringing standardization and competition to even smaller Texas communities.

With the launching of the interstate highway program in 1956, transcontinental travel was forever transformed. Broad, limited-access paths carved through-routes, skirted many communities, and bypassed others miles away. The OST, meandering through downtowns of all sizes, went unused. The era of the mom-and-pop roadside had ended.

In 1950, Currie and Edna Brooks opened the Wes-Tex Courts in Sheffield, which they constructed using native limestone rock. The small neon sign outside the office at right sat beside where the OST curved through Sheffield. They were one of hundreds of similar enterprises launched in the years after World War II, using local materials and adopting Western themes. They successfully ran the courts for over a decade before retiring. (James Collett.)

Others used classic names. The Spanish Trail Lodge of Fort Stockton (built in 1953) recalled the OST heritage, as its 20 units were the average motel size. Though the parking lot remained unpaved, other items essential to Texas motels were present—neon signs and refrigerated air. Many Texas motels, basic rows of standardized cabins, chose dramatic Western names such as Ozona's Silver Spur Ranch Motel or Fort Stockton's Silver Saddle Lodge. (James Collett.)

As more motel operations opened along the OST, owners sought to ensure travelers of the quality of their establishment. One method was to join referral chains—networks promising a standard of quality, identified by special signage. The Ranch Motel in Van Horn, built in 1947, advertised referrals from AAA, Duncan Hines, and the American Motor Hotel Association. (James Collett.)

Founded in 1946, Best Western became the most successful referral chain, operating as an incorporated business. Field representatives inspected member motels, developed national marketing programs, operated a reservation system, and provided distinctive signage for members. Sonora's Western Motel took full advantage with this 1962 version of the company sign. By that date, Best Western was the largest motel chain in the industry. (James Collett.)

For many travelers, the motels they selected were better equipped than their homes and required none of the household chores. Swimming pools, often visibly placed in the central courtyards, became a feature attraction. On the Ranch Motel's postcards, the heated pool took top billing, replacing referral chains. For some small owners, a pool proved expensive advertising for a feature often little used by lodgers. (James Collett.)

As older tourist courts found themselves losing business, many worked to adapt. J.G. and Jewel Childs remodeled their 33-unit Kerrville business (see page 71) into the Del Norte Motel, adding a large neon-lit sign, refrigerated air, televisions, and a swimming pool. Attracting and satisfying overnight travelers became critical to survival. With 40 percent of vacationers returning to places they had stayed before, references frequently defined success or failure. (James Collett.)

Perhaps the most impressive transformation was El Paso's Del Camino (see page 108). By the late 1950s, the Del Camino billed itself as the "world's second largest," with 275 rooms stretching along both sides of Highway 80. There was a complete shopping center, a coffee shop renowned for quality steaks and Mexican food, and even a bullfighting museum. It was the new version of the old Grande Courts concept (see page 60).

The dramatic growth of travelers in the 1950s and the successful proliferation of mom-and-pop motels eventually drew larger investors and the formation of chain facilities with standardized design, franchised to local operators along the OST route. The Fort Stockton Holiday Inn seen here contained all the features of the brand, founded in 1952, including standardized room size and the 50-foot sign, alight with 1,500 feet of neon. (James Collett.)

Ramada Inns, established in 1954, also became common along the OST. The name was the Spanish word for "a shady resting place." Yet, buildings employed an eastern "Williamsburg" architecture, and the primary logo was a friendly bald innkeeper with a suit, top hat, and a red trumpeted banner. Once travelers stepped inside (as here in Van Horn), standardization prevailed. All local identity vanished. (James Collett.)

Travel trailers, around since the early autocamping days, again became popular with many vacationers in the post–World War II years. Trailer parks, offering both overnight and longer-term spaces, provided another small business opportunity. C.R. McGuffey operated the El Rancho Grande park on Highway 80 West in El Paso. A tile bathhouse, laundry room, shade trees, and playground complemented 36 overnight drive-through spaces. (James Collett.)

Small-scale entrepreneurs also established a diverse variety of eating places on the OST roadside. Matchbooks provided a simple advertising tool. Layl's Sandwich Shop of Liberty, with "busy, attractive car hops," was the first of a quarter-mile block of OST dining options, followed by Griffin's Steak House and the Tourist Café, its menus "lipping full of he-man food," and ending with the Ott Grill, "where Greyhounds pull in and out hourly." (James Collett.)

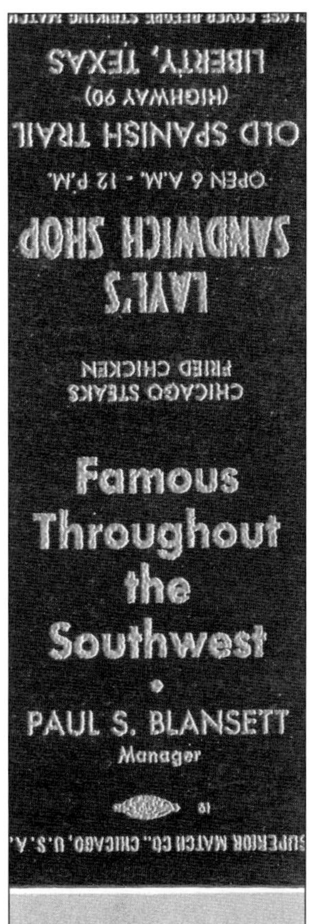

Service stations provided a third roadside opportunity. Franchised through national brands, most stations were locally owned. Albert Hoelscher's Columbus Sinclair station (seen here shortly after opening in 1951) is typical of the oblong-box style that most major companies—Sinclair, Texaco, and Exxon—developed. White buildings with decorative trim and plenty of glass and shiny metal, with standardized signage and a well-lit canopy, created a modern and efficient image. (Nesbitt Memorial Library Archives.)

Older-style stations remained, especially in smaller OST communities, though perhaps adding more brand-name elements. In 1943, former ranch manager Hubert Collett purchased a Texaco station and ranch supply store in Sheffield. When his sons returned from World War II, they worked there for a time. In 1954, Collett sold it, purchasing a newer-style Texaco in Ozona. Pictured are Bill Collett (left) and an unidentified attendant in Texaco uniforms. (James Collett.)

Perhaps the most daring mom-and-pop station was established at the intersection of the Broadway of America and the OST. Along with Chevron gasoline, the Davis Mountain Station had a café and a few old-style courts. For those travelers who had not planned well, it proved a lifesaving oasis. Isolated, with limited appeal, it eventually closed. Today, Interstates 10 and 20 diverge there in a desolate, uninhabited landscape. (James Collett.)

The OST roadside through each town became lined with a mixture of home-grown roadside businesses—motels, restaurants, and service stations. This 1960s segment of Highway 290 through Sonora was a typical example. The photograph includes two motels, two cafes, and a Humble gasoline station. The scene would repeat again and again, with only the names of restaurants, motels, or gasoline brands changing. (Sutton County Historical Society.)

Despite the growing standard view, towns maintained unique elements. Before arriving at this Ozona spot, drivers passed "Silk Stocking Row," a group of mansions erected by ranching families who became rich during the 1920s oil boom. For a time, Ozona had more millionaires per capita than anywhere in the world. Hubert Collett operated the Texaco on the left, built in the 1930s in the Streamline Moderne Art Deco style. (James Collett.)

This 1960s aerial view of Kerrville looking east provides another perspective on the changing roadside. Highway 27 zigzags through downtown just left of the Guadalupe River. The multi-story Blue Bonnet Hotel still dominates downtown. A lack of available real estate led mom-and-pop businesses to develop further from town. The large H-E-B grocery store (bottom center), a long-established business (see page 75), was well-positioned to serve both locals and travelers. (James Collett.)

As the Texas highway system developed, roadways moved from congested downtowns to the outskirts of communities. In 1941, US Highway 90 was paved through Flatonia, seen here. OST segments were eliminated on both ends of town, though the main route still lay along downtown Main Street. Though the war years saw little highway work, they demonstrated a need for an improved interstate network. (E.A. Arnim Archives and Museum.)

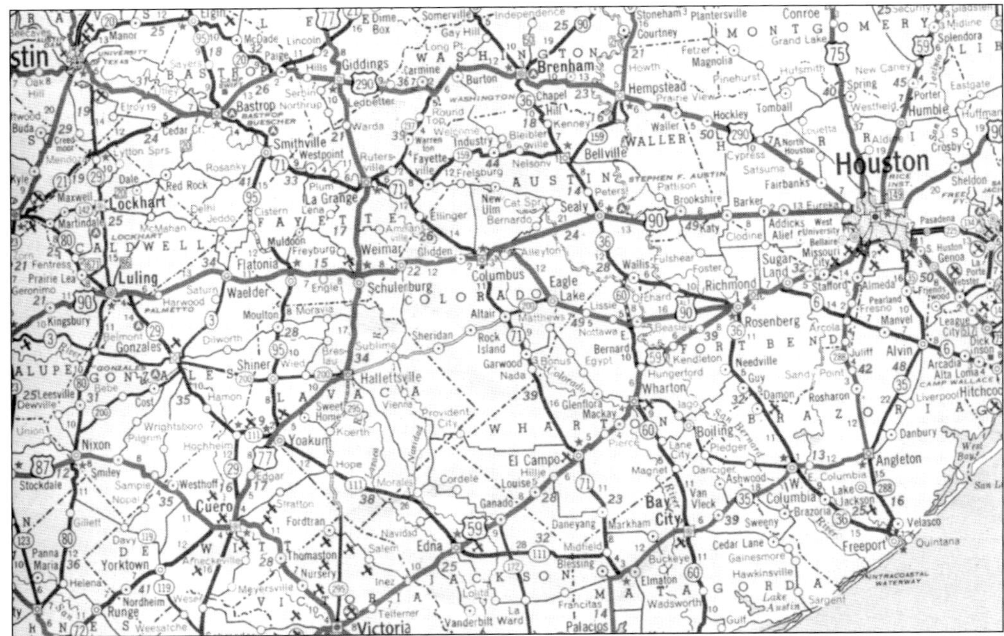

Service stations became major suppliers of roadmaps. This 1940s Sinclair Texas map shows how the old OST route was broken up by changing highway designations. The Houston-to-Columbus segment became Alternate US 90 (a new route running to the north), and the Flatonia-to-Seguin segment through Gonzales became State Highway 3. Few travelers continued to follow the old OST path across East Texas. (James Collett.)

Yet nature sometimes sent travelers back to the old routes. In June 1954, Hurricane Alice caused record-breaking floods that destroyed the Live Oak Creek Bridge near Fort Lancaster (pages 84–85), forcing US Highway 290 traffic to temporarily return to the 1920s Edwards Plateau descent. The same storm caused Johnson Draw to flood through Ozona, killing 14 people and destroying homes and businesses, including Hubert Collett's Texaco. (James Collett.)

Highway improvements proceeded fairly rapidly after the Federal Aid Highway Act of 1956 established the interstate highway system. Interstate 10, largely following the path the OST blazed, was approved by the Bureau of Public Roads in 1959. Construction began that year and continued until 1982. Explosives, bulldozers, and trucks slice through the Hill Country near Junction in this 1970 photograph, carving a broad, direct path across Texas. (Texas Department of Transportation.)

Interstate 10's completion, the growth of motel and dining franchises, and the demise of the service station transformed roadside industries. As demonstrated in this view of businesses along Interstate 10 in Orange, brand names dominated, with Gary's Coffee Shop being perhaps the only local business. For good or bad, the uniquely local, quirky adventure of the original OST roadside was over. (Heritage House Museum.)

Seven

Retracing the Trail

Writing in 1929, Harral Ayres summed up the vision for the Old Spanish Trail: "It was this crusading spirit in half of the counties across the continent that has now opened this automobile artery . . . and the wealth of a great nation is already pouring into it." Interstate 10 dramatically fulfilled that grandiose vision. A multi-lane, limited-access, high-speed river of pavement carries an immeasurable flow of people and freight along the southern transcontinental route.

Yet, that uniform template forever changed the transcontinental road those pioneers built. Each community constructed its piece of the Old Spanish Trail, lining the roadside with businesses essential to automobile travel and tourism and connected to the greater world beyond. For some five decades, many reaped the benefits of their work until the changing roadway reduced them to an exit ramp on the interstate.

Another important element of the OST vision was also lost—the idea of the trail, a connected pathway through a cordon of unique local places. Today's drivers can cross the continent without "touching" anything beyond the standardized. A bit stereotyped by today's ethics, Ayres's vision of experiencing the "Spanish" culture was an early attempt at heritage tourism, the idea of traveling to experience those things—cultural, historical, and natural—that authentically represent the stories and people of a place.

Interest in the Old Spanish Trail has benefited from the growth of highway nostalgia, as drivers seek to rediscover and travel historic roads like the OST. Organizations promote certain routes, automobile clubs conduct special road trips, and individual travelers set out to find and drive a piece of old highway.

Opportunities remain to rediscover the OST. Fragments of the Texas miles can still be found, and sometimes driven. A piece remains in Columbus. Segments wander through the Hill Country around Comfort. Nice stretches cross Crockett and Pecos Counties. The river road still offers a more leisurely entry into El Paso. When driving a quiet, winding stretch of the old highway, one regains a small sense of the more relaxed, unstandardized, eccentric, and unexpected adventure of traveling the early Old Spanish Trail Highway.

Sometimes only photographs remain. In 1979, architectural critic John Margolies captured El Paso's Del Camino in his Roadside America series. Margolies spent 40 years recording roadside structures across the nation. Several lay along the OST. Besides the Del Camino, his photographs include Beaumont's Alamo Plaza Motel, Houston's Chief Motel, and Liberty's Stump Café. The Del Camino was condemned and demolished in 1993. (Library of Congress.)

The OST100 organization formed in 2002 to revive interest in this iconic highway and those adventurous years of early automobile travel. Inspired by the efforts of Charlotte Kahl of San Antonio, historical groups along the route have organized conferences, reenactments, and motorcades (like this 2019 one from San Antonio to Comfort), recalling events from the 1920s, with a 2029 transcontinental motorcade planned as a grand finale. (James Collett.)

A handful of historic bridges remain along the post-1930 OST route, now relegated to state highways or Interstate 10 access roads. The Pecos River Bridge, completed in 1933, is one of 20 remaining examples of the once-common Parker through truss bridge. It remains active along a 20-mile stretch of old OST highway, now State Highway 290, a beautiful drive but without services. As Ayres warned, "Stock up with supplies." (James Collett.)

Many Texas OST communities maintain vestiges of their 1920s and 1930s appearance. Flatonia's heritage program has preserved much of the 1920s look of North Main Street (see page 53), though the Flatonia Motor Company building is gone. Façades may have altered, but traces of old filling stations, grocery stores, restaurants, and motels may still be discovered along original OST routes through towns. (Photograph by Judy Pate.)

In 2010, photographer Carol Highsmith launched her 21st-century America project, a series of high-resolution digital photographs of American communities and countryside as a record of the early 21st century and archived in the Library of Congress. Highsmith's photographs also captured early 20th-century fragments, like this 2014 photograph of the restored Magnolia gasoline station in Gonzales closely resembling the one that operated in Seguin (see page 55). (Library of Congress.)

Carol Highsmith photographed Sierra Blanca's Best Café (see page 104) in 2014, which apparently ended its days as an antique store. Eating establishments along the OST changed owners and names many times over the years. Today's intrepid voyagers willing to try their luck with an unfamiliar local café might follow travel writer William Least Heat Moon's advice—the more calendars on the wall, the better the food. (Library of Congress.)

Among the more unique remaining artifacts of the early OST are two of the original obelisks marking the highway's route through Junction (pages 69–70), now located at Junction's excellent Kimble County Historical Museum, which includes an exhibit on the OST and one on Coke Stevenson, OST leader of the Hill Country section and governor of Texas from 1941 to 1947. (James Collett.)

Finally, on a private ranch beside a stretch of the original gravel and dirt OST, two markers approaching a century in age, with information long weathered away, still point east and west. Astride the original transcontinental route, the San Antonio–San Diego stage road, they provide a reminder that Texas remains, as it has always been, the significant central piece of the southern journey westward. (Warren Nutt.)

Discover Thousands of Local History Books Featuring Millions of Vintage Images

Arcadia Publishing, the leading local history publisher in the United States, is committed to making history accessible and meaningful through publishing books that celebrate and preserve the heritage of America's people and places.

Find more books like this at
www.arcadiapublishing.com

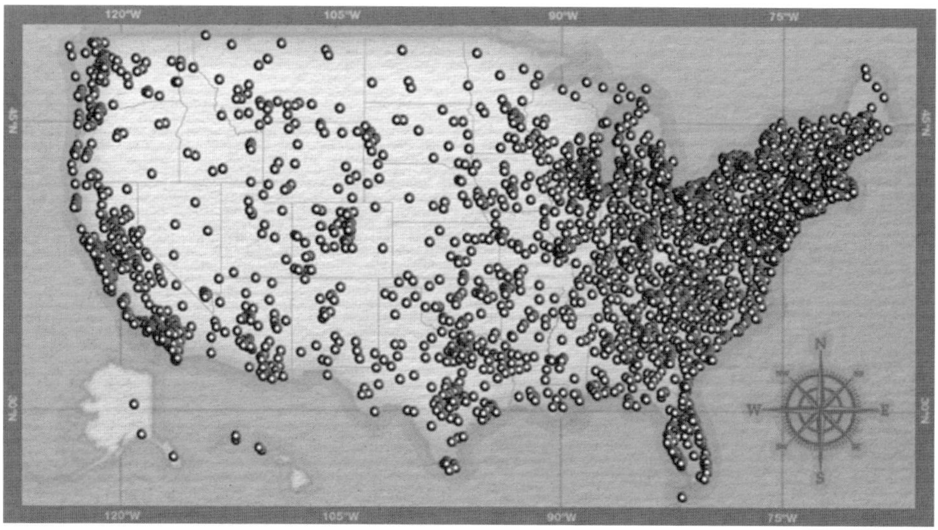

Search for your hometown history, your old stomping grounds, and even your favorite sports team.

Consistent with our mission to preserve history on a local level, this book was printed in South Carolina on American-made paper and manufactured entirely in the United States. Products carrying the accredited Forest Stewardship Council (FSC) label are printed on 100 percent FSC-certified paper.